Crime and Criminal Justice
in Scotland

Crime and Criminal Justice in Scotland

Peter Young

Centre for Law and Society
University of Edinburgh

EDINBURGH: THE STATIONERY OFFICE

© The Stationery Office Limited 1997
The Stationery Office Limited
South Gyle Crescent, Edinburgh EH12 9EB

Application for reproduction should be made to The Stationery Office Limited

First published 1997

British Library Cataloguing in Publication Data
A catalogue record for this book is available from the British Library

ISBN 0 11 495808 4

CONTENTS

Acknowledgements

A number of individuals made a significant contribution to the completion of this book. Bernadette Monaghan helped to prepare the final text and made valuable suggestions in the process; Rebecca Sawyer prepared the Glossary and also helped by indicating where the text could be improved. Dr J. Curran and Dr J. Tombs of The Scottish Office Central Research Unit provided support and encouragement throughout what has turned out to be a lengthy project. Maureen Young deserves particular thanks for setting up the now very large database, on which the text is based, together with Professor F. H. McClintock. She has since provided advice and help at every stage.

NOTE ON STATISTICAL SOURCES

The statistical sources from which most of the figures used in this book are derived are the *Statistical Bulletins* which form part of what is now called the *Criminal Justice Series*, published annually (normally) by The Scottish Office, and their equivalent predecessor volumes. The volumes most heavily relied upon are now called *Recorded Crime in Scotland* (Serial number CrJ/date/2), *Homicide in Scotland* (CrJ/date/5), *Prisons Statistics Scotland* (CrJ/date/6) and *Criminal Proceedings in Scottish Courts* (CRJ/date/7). Where figures are derived from other sources, these are named in the text. The figures for Chapter 9 are from *Referrals of Children to Reporters and Children's Hearings* (SWK/CH/date/19), a *Statistical Bulletin* in the *Social Work Series* published by The Scottish Office. Numbers in the text have been rounded as appropriate.

INTRODUCTION

This book has three aims. The first and most important is to provide a readily available, introductory overview of the criminal justice system in Scotland, together with a broad picture of the main trends in recorded crimes and offences. Conceived in this way, the book is aimed at the general public and tries to put together, for the first time in a single publication, a 'short guide' to one of the more important, characteristically Scottish, of those institutions that affect our daily lives. It should be seen primarily in this context as a source of public information. In addition, the book may also serve as a contribution to a more informed public debate on this area of very great importance. It is not simply that the control of crime costs the public a substantial sum of money each year, but, perhaps what is more important, that crime, and the efforts made to control it, directly affect the quality of life. In the consideration of such an important matter, knowledge must be preferable to ignorance; it is hoped that this book may be of help by presenting in an open and straightforward manner what can otherwise seem to be a mass of complex facts and figures.

These two purposes set the tone of what follows; the pursuit of them has led to an avoidance of jargon and, wherever possible, the avoidance also of technical legal vocabulary. Where examples of both have been inevitable, terms are explained when first introduced. There is also a Glossary.

Although this book has been conceived mainly with the general public in mind, it also makes a contribution to the academic debate. It is based on a considerable volume of research, much of it started under the direction of the late and much missed Professor F. H. McClintock, conducted in the Centre for Law and Society, at the University of Edinburgh, over a number of years with the support of The Scottish Office Home Department. In this context, the book ought to be of some interest to scholars undertaking the comparative study of legal systems. For, while it seems to be known that Scotland has its own distinctive criminal law that differs in many respects from that of England and Wales, few seem to be well versed in what Scots criminal law or its institutions of criminal justice are actually like. Such ignorance may well be attributable to the small number of readily available publications; with the publication of this book, it is hoped that this ignorance will be a thing of the past.

From time to time in the text, comparisons are made with patterns of crime and criminal justice in England and Wales. These are for illustrative purposes; no comparisons are made with the separate criminal justice system of Northern Ireland.

Chapter 1

◆

THE CRIMINAL JUSTICE SYSTEM IN CONTEXT

The United Kingdom is a unitary state, but is unusual in that it contains three legal systems; that of Scotland, and those of England and Wales and of Northern Ireland. While the law of Northern Ireland is similar to that of England and Wales, the law of Scotland is different. It is also administered through legal institutions which are indigenous and differ in important respects from those found elsewhere. The distinctive nature of Scots law and legal institutions is particularly marked in its criminal law – the part of the law which deals with acts (or failure to act in certain circumstances) which may be prosecuted in the criminal courts and be punished by the imposition of penal sanctions, such as fines or imprisonment.

There are two main purposes to this first chapter. The first is to describe some of the main ways in which the criminal law of Scotland and its criminal justice system are distinctive. Rather than providing a detailed description of each stage of the criminal process, the chapter concentrates on two features which are of particular importance: the common law nature of Scots criminal law, and its system of public prosecution. The first is fundamental because it is at the very heart of how Scots lawyers perceive the system within which they work; the idea of criminal law as common law is an essential part of their conception of the law's 'tradition'. It is one of those factors which creates the sense of cultural continuity and coherence which makes it possible to talk of a distinctive Scottish system. The second feature is fundamental because it is the public prosecutor, particularly the procurator fiscal, who is central to the smooth running of the criminal justice system. It is the 'fiscal' who makes many of the key decisions: the decision to prosecute, how the prosecution will proceed and the court in which the case will be heard. The fiscal is also in formal control of the police investigation of crimes and is central to the promotion of new developments such as mediation and reparation, as well as alternatives to prosecution.

The second main purpose is to provide an overview of the criminal justice system, partly to introduce vocabulary but also to place it in a historical and a comparative context. An appreciation of the comparative context is important because, although it is proper to stress the ways in which the Scottish system is distinct, it would be misleading to leave the impression that every aspect of Scottish criminal justice is unique.

The Historical Context

Until 1707, Scotland was an independent state with its own parliament in Edinburgh which made laws separately from the parliament of England and Wales. In that year, however, both these parliaments enacted legislation (the 'Acts of Union') which created a new political entity, the United Kingdom of Great Britain. One very important result of this legislation was the establishment of a new parliament, located in London, with powers to make laws for all of the states which henceforth were to comprise the United Kingdom; and this remains the position today. Another very important aspect of the Acts of Union was the provision of safeguards to protect three key Scottish institutions: the educational system, the Church and the legal system, all of which, as a result, have continued to develop separately from their equivalents in England and Wales.

These safeguards were, no doubt, partly the product of political compromise in that they put limits on the assimilation of a small country by a larger, more powerful close neighbour; but they reflected also genuine and deep differences in traditions and in the design of institutions. Scotland not only possessed, for example, a different court structure from England and Wales, but its law had developed from sources which sometimes overlapped with those of England and Wales but which were often separate and distinct. As a result, the two legal systems had, generally speaking, significant differences of outlook and approach.

The modern legal system in Scotland should be viewed in this historical context. While since 1707 there has been some convergence between the two systems, especially in some areas where one can talk of there being a common 'UK' law (commercial law is an example), many differences still remain and this is particularly true of their criminal law, where the two systems diverge in fundamental respects.

The Criminal Law of Scotland as Common Law

One of the notable characteristics of much of Scots criminal law is that it is what lawyers call common law and, in this, it contrasts not only with much of the criminal law of England and Wales, but also with that of many of the other member states of the European Community. In these countries the criminal law is said to be codified. This means that the definitions of crimes and offences are set down in texts which, in continental Europe, are actually called 'codes'. It is not at all unusual for a country to have up to five codes which cover the whole of its law (a criminal code, a civil code, a penal code, a commercial law code and so on). Although in England and Wales, there are no codes as such, much of the criminal law is defined in statutes – that is, in Acts of parliament which come into force only after they have received full parliamentary scrutiny. In contrast, much of Scots criminal law is not the product of legislation; rather, the definitions of crimes arise from successive decisions of the criminal courts or from the writings of highly respected legal authors, known as the institutional writers, whose views are accorded authoritative status by the courts, by legal scholars and the profession alike. Common law crimes include the most serious, such as murder, robbery, rape, assault, theft and fraud, as well as the less serious, such as breach of the peace.

There are areas of Scots criminal law, however, which are contained in statutes, and these are growing in number. Some of these statutory defined crimes are of considerable importance such as the laws defining the illegal use of drugs. Furthermore, many of these crimes are defined in the same way as in England and Wales: for example, road traffic law, and laws relating to environmental pollution and computer misuse. These are all types of behaviour which are more 'modern', and some of them, such as drug dealing and computer fraud, have an increasingly international dimension.

The distinction between common law crimes and those defined by statute is of some importance as it affects the process of sentencing upon a finding of guilt. Theoretically, the penalty for any common law crime or offence can be life imprisonment. Of course, this will rarely happen as the actual sentence given in a particular case will be limited by a number of factors including the sentencing powers of the court in which the case is being heard. But the common law base of Scots criminal law is important here as it leaves the judge in such crimes with a very wide discretionary power to determine each sentence. Although some commentators regard this wide discretion as a matter of concern, others see it as a positive virtue of the system. It is said to be a matter of concern as it leaves too much room for possible inequalities in sentencing to creep in; it is regarded as a virtue because it allows the judge to adapt the decision to the special features of the case being considered.

Whichever side one comes down on in this particular argument, what is clear is that the common law basis of Scots criminal law is one of its most notable features. It is basic to the system and lends to the law the characteristic of great flexibility, a feature which codified systems do not possess to the same degree. This flexibility in turn leads to considerable adaptability which means that the criminal law can be developed without recourse to legislation which is both costly and time-consuming. In theory this means that the criminal justice system can respond to 'new' situations quickly by an existing common law crime being made to cover a form of behaviour which is causing concern, such as happened when, in 1984, the common law offence of reckless conduct was used as the basis for the prosecution of shopkeepers who were supplying glue-sniffing kits to children. Another, more recent example, is the creation, by the High Court, of the crime of rape in marriage.

The System of Public Prosecution

As was said earlier, Scotland possesses a system of public prosecution, and the conduct of a prosecution is in the hands of a public official. The head of the prosecution service is the Lord Advocate, who is a member of the government, but the day-to-day running of the system is devolved, in particular, to the procurator fiscal, whose role is described in greater depth in Chapter 4.

Scotland is not the only country which has a public prosecutor. Indeed, most other countries in Europe also have public prosecution systems. Nevertheless, the procurator fiscal is a crucial part of the Scottish system of criminal justice. The procurator fiscal makes key decisions: whether to prosecute, in what court the prosecution will take place and what type of procedure is likely to be used. The fiscal is also formally in charge of the conduct of the investigation of crimes and can therefore ask the police to follow up certain lines of enquiry. The fiscal has additional responsibilities relating to the investigation of sudden deaths and complaints against the police.

It is the power to make these decisions which places the fiscal at the heart of the system. In organisational terms, the fiscal 'bridges' the early investigatory parts of the criminal process to the later judicial ('judging') stages and is very much in control of who and what is allowed to cross that bridge. To use a concept developed in Chapter 3, the procurator fiscal is a key, perhaps *the* key, 'gatekeeper' to the system.

The Scottish System in a Comparative Context

Legal scholars sometimes divide legal systems into types or families. It is said that there are two predominant families of legal system in the Western world; these are the civilian systems, derived from the law of Rome, and the common law systems, derived from English law. These are general classifications which are not intended to account for every aspect of a particular country's law. On this basis, however, lawyers do class a country's legal system as belonging more to one classification than to another. Most of the legal systems of western Europe are said to belong to the first of these families, the civilian system, whereas the legal systems of most of the old British Empire and those of most US states (except Louisiana) are said to belong to the common law tradition. There are a number of countries, Scotland being one of them, that are classified as 'mixed' systems: that is, the legal system bears the imprint of both families of law.

The difference between these two families lies in their

distinctive patterns of historical development. The civilian systems developed under the influence of Roman law principles as taught in the universities of Europe from the twelfth century onwards. The common law systems developed much more on the basis of 'judge-made' law. It is argued that these historical differences have resulted in distinct legal outlooks as well as distinct legal institutions: the civilian lawyer is said to reason from general principles and general rules to particular cases, while the common law lawyer is said to work more pragmatically.

While these generalisations are helpful in pointing to differences between legal systems, they are less helpful when applied to particular branches of law, such as the criminal law. For example, while much of Scots private or civil law may be related (now distantly) to Roman law, the same cannot be said, as we have seen, of its criminal law with its common law base. There are, however, aspects of the Scottish criminal justice system that are akin to the civilian systems of Europe, especially its public prosecution system.

Institutions, Procedures and Policy

While the common law base of the criminal law of Scotland and the procurator fiscal constitute the key features of the criminal justice system, there are also other ways in which the Scottish system is different. As will be seen in Chapter 3, there are certain pre-trial procedures in Scotland that differ significantly from those found, for example, in England and Wales. Again, uniquely, there are three verdicts possible as the outcome to criminal trials in Scotland. Furthermore, and looking beyond the criminal justice system in the narrow sense, there exists a distinctive system of juvenile justice in Scotland known as the Children's Hearings. It differs from most other Western juvenile justice systems, not just in that it is 'decriminalised' – that is, it is not a criminal court – but also in the degree to which it has retained a clear welfare emphasis. There are also some aspects of the adult penal system in Scotland which differ from those in England and Wales. Social work services for criminal justice in Scotland, for example, are both organised differently from in England and Wales – there is no separate probation service in Scotland – and there are aspects of policy which are distinctive. The same may be said to be true also of the organisation of the prison system and of the policies which guide it.

While it is the aim of this book to note these differences, this is not its main one. Rather, the main objective is to describe the Scottish criminal justice system in an open manner to show how it has developed and how it works. Comparisons with other systems are relevant only in as much as they help in this main purpose; they can all too easily be misleading, especially when they concentrate only on differences. For while there is much about the Scottish system which is distinctive, there is more that is shared in common with other systems in the Western world, in terms of both its institutional structure and its policies.

Chapter 2

$\blacklozenge$

TRENDS IN CRIMES AND OFFENCES

The purpose of this chapter is to provide information on the incidence of recorded crimes and offences in Scotland for the period 1950–95. The aim is to portray general trends rather than to examine detailed changes in the occurrence of each recorded crime and every offence. In order, however, to give some idea of the current position, a more detailed breakdown of changes in the incidence of certain selected crimes and offences from 1980 to 1995 is provided. The crimes and offences selected for this more detailed examination are those which are either the most commonly recorded or which are of particular seriousness.

Before beginning this analysis, it may be useful to describe the sources of information from which the data in this chapter are derived. The data are taken from two types of statistics published by the government. In the earlier sections of the chapter, the statistics used are taken from a statistical bulletin called *Recorded Crime in Scotland*. This statistical bulletin is published annually as part of The Scottish Office *Criminal Justice Series*. In the later part of the chapter, the statistics are taken from another source known as the *National Crime Survey*, the results of which are published periodically. These sources of data give different but complementary measures of the amount and nature of crime in Scotland. Each source has some advantages and some limitations. An outline of these is given to enhance the discussion that follows.

Recorded Crime in Scotland

The central problem with these statistics on crime is acknowledged to be that they do not record all the crimes and offences that are committed in Scotland. Rather, these statistics only reveal those crimes and offences which come to the notice of the police and which the police record. For this reason, these statistics on crime are said to be based on 'crimes (and offences) recorded by the police'. This is why these published data are called 'recorded crime'; they are sometimes also known as 'the police statistics', to indicate their main source.

A number of factors will influence whether a criminal event actually ends up being recorded as a crime or offence in these statistics. Generally speaking, there are two ways in which the police get to know of a criminal event – either it is reported to them or they come across it in the course of performing their duties. Research has revealed that the most common way the police get to know of a crime is through the first of these routes, when either an individual or an organisation makes a decision to tell the police that they have been the victim of a crime or have what they think is knowledge of a crime that has been, or is being, committed. Many things can affect whether a criminal event is reported to the police. Research has shown that many crimes go unreported because individuals think the matter is too trivial (many acts of vandalism are said to be regarded in this way), because they are scared or because they find it too painful to make a report (some sexual crimes are said to fall into this category). As a result, there is considerable under-reporting of crime. Recent estimates suggest that less than half of all criminal incidents in Scotland are reported to the police by victims and that, with particularly sensitive crimes, such as sexual offences, the figure may be as low as 15 per cent. In contrast, some crimes, however, are known to have a very high rate of reporting. This may be because they are of a serious nature, as with murder, or because the decision to report is a necessary first stage in the victims trying to recover some of the costs that have been incurred. Two such crimes are car theft and housebreaking, where it is normally a condition of an insurance claim that a report is made to the police.

It can be seen from these examples that many separate decisions have to be taken before a particular criminal incident is reported to the police in the first place. There are, thereafter, another series of decisions to be made by the police themselves as to whether to record the incident at all and, if so, how to record it. The police, for example, may decide either that an event that is reported to them is not a crime or that there is insufficient evidence to be sure that a crime has occurred. In the first example, the police cannot record the event as a crime in any circumstances, and in the second example, a record is unlikely to be made until more evidence is made available; and this, of course, may not be forthcoming.

These examples show that the statistics do not record all the crime that is committed in Scotland but, rather, are the end product of a complex chain of decision-making. Most importantly, the examples show that there is considerable under-reporting and under-recording of crime and, therefore, that there is a gap between the situation as described by the statistics and the 'real' incidence of criminality. The difference between the total of crimes committed and those recorded is known as 'the dark figure' of crime. It is this 'dark figure' of crime that must be taken into account when making any claims about the state of crime in Scotland.

Although the 'dark figure' of crime is probably the most important limitation of the recorded statistics on crime, there are also others. These are concerned not so much with the issue of accuracy and coverage as with the interpretation of the data once they are published. There are two matters in particular to be mentioned. The first concerns changes in 'reporting and recording practices'. As was seen above, the question of reporting is central to the process of recording, and it follows, therefore, that any change in the manner in which crime is reported will have an effect on the final picture. Although it is the public who report most crimes to the police, it is generally thought that changes in the general public's reporting practice are slow. In contrast, any change in the recording practice of the police themselves can have an immediate effect on the statistics. If, for example, the police were to decide automatically to record all reports they receive of a particular crime, this could substantially alter the picture in that it would cause a sudden apparent change in the incidence of the crime. Or, to look at another slightly different example, police forces, from time to time, quite legitimately may decide to enforce a particular crime more strictly; the effect of this deployment of manpower will mean that this crime will show a sudden 'jump' in the recorded crime statistics without there being any real increase in the actual incidence of the crime in society.

Abrupt changes in the statistics can also be caused by other changes as well as those in reporting and recording practices. Occasionally, changes occur in the way in which the recorded crime statistics themselves are organised. The recorded crime statistics are normally presented by grouping individual crimes into broader classes, categories or groups for statistical purposes. In *Recorded Crime in Scotland*, for example, there are five groups of crimes and two of offences. Each of these groups is made up of a number of individual crimes or offences. The group known as 'non-sexual crimes of violence' (or violence) has a number of crimes in it, which range from murder and, culpable homicide to serious assault and causing death by dangerous driving. Occasionally, the way in which these broad classes are defined can change, or a particular crime can be moved from one class to another. When either or both of these rare things happen, it can have an effect on the statistics by making it seem as though a significant change in the distribution of crime has taken place. Such a reordering of the criminal statistics took place in the Scottish statistics in 1978 when the classification, which had been in place since 1897 without great change, was altered. One consequence of this is to make the comparison of crimes over time more difficult; this accounts for the way in which some of the statistics are presented below where it has been necessary to show both the old and the new classifications on the same graphs for the sake of completeness.

The five groups of crimes and two groups of offences listed in *Recorded Crime in Scotland* are: non-sexual crimes of violence (or violence); crimes of indecency (or indecency); crimes of dishonesty (or dishonesty); fire-raising, vandalism, etc.; other crimes; miscellaneous offences; and motor vehicle offences.

Before examining the advantages and limitations of the other source of data (*the National Crime Survey*), an analysis of recorded crimes and offences from 1950 onwards will be presented.

Recorded Crimes and Offences in Scotland, 1950–95

This section analyses the main trends in recorded crimes and offences for the period 1950–95.

Figure 2.1 shows changes in the pattern of all crimes and offences added together as well as for crimes and offences separately. The graph has been complicated by the change in the classification of crimes and offences in 1978 referred to above. As can be seen, the general effect of this resulted in an increase in

Figure 2.1   Crimes and offences recorded by the police, 1950–95.

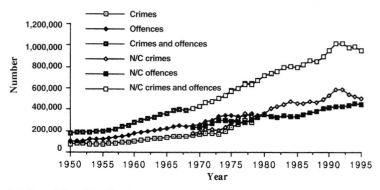

N/C =   New Classifications, 1978 onwards.
Source: Recorded Crime in Scotland.

the number of crimes recorded and a decrease in the number of offences recorded (although it must be stressed that the number of offences now exceeds the 1978 level). Although the reclassification has had this amplifying effect on crimes, it is clear that it has not altered the general trend which had been established: recorded crimes appear to be increasing at a faster rate than recorded offences.

The general position described by Figure 2.1 is of a significant rise in recorded crimes and offences throughout this period from just below 200,000 in 1950 to 955,000 crimes and offences in 1995. This represents just under a fivefold increase in recorded crimes and offences over the period. Careful examination will, however, show that the rate of increase in crimes and offences has varied over time. The first period of significant increase begins in the mid-1950s and lasts until the mid-1960s, after which there is a short plateau before the upward trend continues, with small dips in the mid-1970s and mid-1980s. There has been, however, a decrease in recorded crime from 1991 to 1995. In 1991 there were 593,000 recorded crimes, compared to 503,000 in 1995, a 15 per cent decline. Recorded offences continued to increase in number until 1994 when they reached a high point of 464,000; but by 1995 the figure had fallen to 452,000, a 3 per cent decrease.

The general pattern of increase described by the line for all recorded crimes and offences is typical in many respects to that experienced in other Western criminal justice systems. Most Western societies have had substantial increases in recorded crimes and offences since the end of the Second World War. The date at which this begins tends to be the mid-1950s, especially in the years 1953–5. The explanation of this pattern is not yet clear. It does appear, however, that there exist long-term patterns in recorded crime. If allowance is made for the unsettling effects of the Second World War, which appear to have caused a substantial increase in recorded crime during the war years, followed by a decrease in the early 1950s, then the rise thereafter seems to be a continuation of a long-term increase which started in the mid- to late 1930s. This followed a long-term decrease in crime from the late Victorian period until the 1930s, with the 1930s as a turning point.

Although the long-term patterns of recorded crime in Scotland thus seem to be similar to those elsewhere, there are some short-term differences which are worthy of note. As will be seen, there is some evidence, for example, that the rate of increase in crime in Scotland from the early to mid-1980s until the early 1990s was significantly slower than that in England and Wales during the same period and, as has been noted, there has been a recent and notable drop in the number of recorded crimes in Scotland from 1991–2 onwards. There has been a similar development in England and Wales. Before examining these recent changes in more detail, it is necessary to return to Figure 2.1 to look at the position for recorded crimes and offences separately.

Examination of the separate lines for crimes and offences during the period from 1950 to 1995 shows that, while both describe an overall increase, the rate of acceleration is, as was noted, greater in the case of crimes, especially after the early 1970s. From that date, crimes seem to have grown at a significantly faster rate than offences, finally exceeding them in number in about 1975. This upswing seems, at least in part, to have been the result of an alteration of recording practice by the police. In 1975, the police in Scotland underwent a major reorganisation. The number of forces was reduced to form eight larger ones, and one result of this was the introduction of standardised recording practices, the effect of which, as the annual recorded statistics noted, was to cause a 'sharp increase in the statistics of crime when compared to previous years' (Criminal statistics, 1975, p. 5).

Figure 2.2 describes the increase in recorded crimes and offences expressed as a rate per 1,000 of the population. The point of examining the statistics in this way is to take account of the demographic changes which occurred over the period.

As this figure shows, the rate of recorded crimes and offences has increased significantly between 1950 and 1995, from just below 40 per 1,000 to 186 per 1,000 of the population. This represents just under a fivefold increase in the rate of recorded crimes and offences per 1,000 of the population.

The Distribution of Crimes and Offences

This section analyses the types of crimes and offences most commonly recorded in Scotland in 1995. Figure 2.3 records the overall distribution of recorded crimes and offences in 1995.

Figure 2.2 Crimes and offences recorded by the police, expressed as a rate per 1,000 of the population, 1950–95.

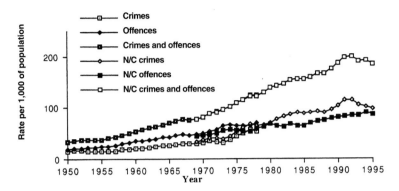

N/C = New Classifications, 1978 onwards.
Source: Recorded Crime in Scotland.

Figure 2.3 Crimes and offences recorded by the police, 1995.

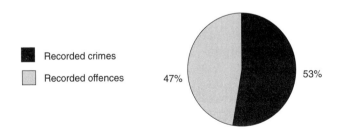

Source: Recorded Crime in Scotland

19

It will be remembered that the recorded crime statistics in Scotland are grouped into five of crimes and two of offences. As can be seen from Figure 2.3, approximately 53 per cent of the recorded total are crimes and about 47 per cent are offences. In some ways this is surprising as it appears to indicate that there are more serious crimes recorded in society than there are less serious offences. It has to be said, however, that many of the actual events recorded as crimes are of a relatively minor nature. Also, the statistics exclude the most common of the recorded offences that are dealt with by the criminal justice system, that is stationary motor vehicle offences (mostly parking), of which there were approximately 460,000 in 1995.

Figure 2.4 describes the distribution between the various groups of recorded crimes and offences. As can be seen, the largest group of all is composed of recorded crimes of dishonesty,

Figure 2.4   The distribution of recorded crimes and offences, 1995.

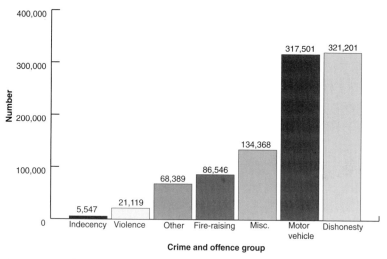

Source: Recorded Crime in Scotland

20

which account for 34 per cent of all recorded crimes and offences; this is followed by motor vehicle offences (33 per cent), miscellaneous offences (13 per cent), fire-raising and vandalism (9 per cent), other crimes (7 per cent), crimes of violence (2 per cent) and crimes of indecency (1 per cent). This makes clear the extent to which the most numerous type of recorded crime in Scotland is property related. Crimes of dishonesty mostly involve housebreaking and the theft of property or valuables – often a car, or property from a car. It also shows the relatively small size of the other four groups of recorded crime which, added together, account for only 19 per cent of all recorded crimes and offences. In comparison (with the exception of crimes of dishonesty), the two groups of recorded offences are much larger, particularly motor vehicle offences, the majority of which in 1995 were related to unlawful use of vehicles. One important conclusion to be drawn here is the extent to which crimes and offences against cars and other motor vehicles figure large in the picture. If the number of recorded crimes of dishonesty (mostly theft of or from a car) are added together with recorded motor vehicle offences, they make up 67 per cent of the total.

The general pattern of crime has been described. It will now be useful to examine crimes and offences separately to build up a more detailed picture.

Recorded Crimes

Figure 2.5 provides a breakdown of the separate groups of recorded crime. The largest group is crimes of dishonesty which account for 64 per cent of all recorded crimes. The individual crimes which comprise this group are housebreaking (23 per cent); other theft (includes theft of pedal cycles) (27 per cent); theft by opening lockfast places (mostly theft from cars) (21 per cent); theft of motor vehicles (12 per cent); shoplifting (9 per

Figure 2.5   The distribution of recorded crimes, 1995.

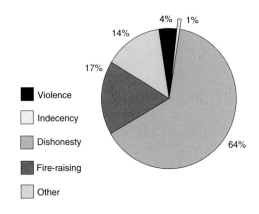

Source: Recorded Crime in Scotland.

cent); fraud (5 per cent); and others (includes forgery, reset and embezzlement) (3 per cent). As will be seen below, there have been significant changes in the number of recorded crimes of dishonesty since 1992 which have affected the overall level of recorded crime in Scotland.

The next largest group of recorded crimes is fire-raising, vandalism, etc., of which vandalism etc. is the most numerous, accounting for 96 per cent, which includes malicious mischief and reckless conduct with firearms. The remainder of this crime group is composed of fire-raising.

The group of 'other crimes' is made up of crimes against public justice (64 per cent), drug offences (36 per cent) and other crimes (conspiracy and explosives offences) (less than 1 per cent). The number of recorded drug offences has increased noticeably in recent years. There was, for example, a 28 per cent increase in this offence between 1994 (19,300) and 1995 (24,800). This increase was related to increased police activity.

Although in numerical terms it is small, the group of non-sexual crimes of violence (or simply violence) contains the most serious crimes recorded by the police. It is made up of robbery (25 per cent), handling offensive weapons (31 per cent), serious assault etc. (33 per cent) and 'other' (11 per cent). The 'other' category includes cruel and unnatural treatment of children, while the serious assault category comprises murder, culpable homicide (including the statutory crime of causing death by dangerous driving), serious assault and attempted murder. There was a 22 per cent increase in recorded crimes of handling offensive weapons between 1994 (5,300) and 1995 (6,500).

Detailed statistics relating to homicide are presented in a separate statistical bulletin called *Homicide in Scotland*. In 1994, there were 108 recorded homicide cases. Of these, 104 were solved (66 were recorded as murder and 38 as culpable homicide). Only 4 cases were recorded as unsolved. Since 1984, the number of recorded cases of all homicides has fluctuated between a low of 79, in 1985 and 1986, to a high of 131 in 1992. The most common method of killing is by use of a sharp instrument, and the most common motive reported was rage or a quarrel. Seventy-eight per cent of victims in 1994 were killed by unemployed persons. The relationship of the main accused to the victim differed significantly by gender. In the case of male victims, 61 per cent were killed by an acquaintance, and 60 per cent of female victims were killed by their partner. Almost half of those accused of homicides recorded in 1994 were aged between 16 and 25.

The final group of recorded crimes, sexual crimes, is also small but, again, comprises some of the most serious crimes. The proper title of this group is 'crimes of indecency' (or indecency). The separate crimes which make up the group are sexual assault (rape, assault with intent to ravish, indecent assault) (30 per cent), lewd and libidinous practices (indecent behaviour towards children, and indecent exposure) (43 per cent), and 'other' which includes prostitution (28 per cent). There was a 10 per cent decrease between 1994 and 1995 in recorded cases of lewd and libidinous practices, but a 2 per cent increase in cases of sexual assault.

Recorded Offences

The two groups of recorded offences are divided into miscellaneous offences (30 per cent) and motor vehicle offences (70 per cent). Together, the two comprise 451,869 offences (or 46 per cent of all crimes and offences). Figures 2.6 and 2.7 record the separate offences which make up each group and the distribution of them within each group.

Although the offences recorded in both figures are relatively minor, they are nevertheless of considerable importance as they

Figure 2.6   The distribution of recorded motor vehicle offences, 1995.

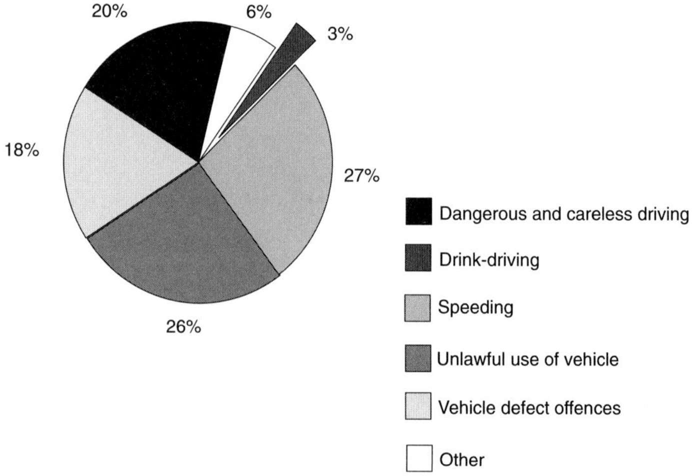

Source: Recorded Crime in Scotland.

impose a heavy burden of work on the criminal justice system and also constitute the type of behaviour that impinges significantly on the public's daily lives. For example, while individual occurrences of offences such as drunkenness and breach of the peace may not be especially damaging, their incidence is the sort of nuisance or 'incivility' that can lower the quality of life, especially if they become concentrated in particular areas. This is true also of the offences recorded within the motor vehicle offences group but here, in addition to nuisance value, there is the added issue of potential danger. As evidence of this, the government has recently introduced new offences related to drink-driving. Also, the maximum penalty for careless or drunken driving has been increased from 5 to 10 years, which clearly shows that these offences are regarded far more seriously than they were a decade ago. The considerable size of this group of offences reinforces the point made earlier concerning the

Figure 2.7   The distribution of recorded miscellaneous offences, 1995.

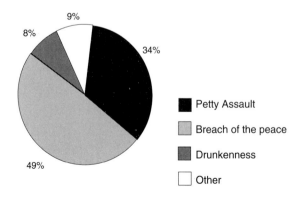

Source: Recorded Crime in Scotland.

amount of crime that is connected, directly or indirectly, with motor vehicles.

1980–95

This section will consider the changes that have occurred in recorded crime in the period from 1980 to 1995. It will be remembered from Figure 2.1 that the incidence of recorded crimes and offences rose throughout this decade, but that the curve describing the pattern of increase in the crimes was somewhat uneven, showing increases and downturns over the period, with a marked decrease in the period from 1992 onwards. To understand why this is so, it is necessary to look in more detail at changes in the incidence of recorded crimes of dishonesty. This is because this group of crimes comprises the largest of all the groups of recorded crime, which means that changes in this group have a very significant impact upon patterns in the overall distribution. Figures 2.8 and 2.9 give a more detailed breakdown of changes within this group.

As Figure 2.8 shows, while the total number of recorded crimes of dishonesty has grown significantly, it is clear that this has been uneven. The largest increases took place in the first years, 1980–1, and then in particular between 1989 and 1991. In comparison, between 1982 and 1989, there was relative stability. Since 1992 there has been a noticeable fall in this group of recorded crimes which has, in turn, contributed to a decrease in the total number of recorded crimes in Scotland.

More detailed examination of Figure 2.9 shows that it was increases in three specific crimes which account for the initial growth, and a decrease in two of these and one other that explains the slower rate in the later years. The three crimes which account for the initial increase are housebreaking, theft by opening a lockfast place, and other theft; each of these crimes continues to

Figure 2.8 Total crimes of dishonesty recorded by the police, 1980–95.

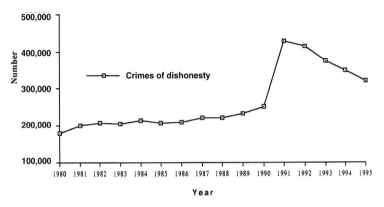

Source: Recorded Crime in Scotland.

Figure 2.9 Crimes of dishonesty recorded by the police, 1980–95.

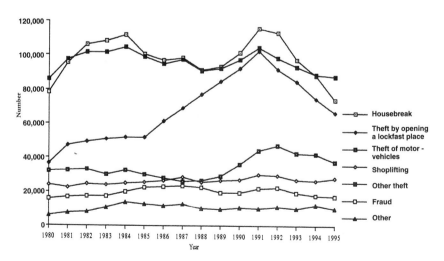

Source: Recorded Crime in Scotland.

27

grow until 1985 when the first and the last begin to decline until 1988 after which they start to increase again; theft by opening lockfast places increases throughout the period until 1991 when it begins to drop. The other crime which begins to decline in number after 1985 until 1988 is theft of motor vehicles.

The more recent decrease from 1992 onwards is accounted for by a decline in the number of housebreakings, thefts by opening lockfast places, other thefts and fraud. Between 1994 and 1995, recorded crimes of dishonesty fell by 8 per cent. This followed decreases of 7 per cent between 1993 and 1994 and 10 per cent between 1992 and 1993. In 1995, there were decreases in six of the seven sub-categories in this group of crimes of dishonesty, the largest falls being in recorded cases of housebreaking and theft by opening lockfast places. The number of recorded cases of housebreaking fell by 16 per cent between 1994 and 1995 and the level is now below that of 1978. The only sub-category in which there was an increase was in recorded crimes of shoplifting.

These recent changes in the level of recorded crimes of dishonesty can be viewed in the medium to longer term. Property-related crime has fallen as a proportion of all recorded crime over the last decade. In 1986, these crimes amounted to 91 per cent of all recorded crime, but in 1995, they comprised 81 per cent, a fall of 10 per cent. It is, therefore, this fall in recorded crimes of dishonesty which explains the fall in the overall level of recorded crime that has been experienced in Scotland.

National Crime Surveys

It was mentioned earlier that the data on crime recorded by the police – such as have been used so far in this chapter – are now complemented by other data gathered by national crime surveys. One purpose of these surveys is to overcome some of the limitations in the data recorded by the police, especially the 'dark figure' of crime – those crimes and offences which go unrecorded in the police statistics. The surveys take the form of large-scale surveys in which people are asked directly about their recent experiences of victimisation and their perceptions of crime and policing and related topics. There have been three national surveys to date involving Scotland. In 1982 and 1988, Scotland participated in the British Crime Survey which was co-ordinated by the Home Office. The 1993 survey in Scotland, however, was designed and co-ordinated by the Central Research Unit of The Scottish Office. It differed from the earlier surveys in that it covered the whole of mainland Scotland together with the larger islands. In the previous surveys, the research interviews were limited to southern and central Scotland.

These large-scale surveys are undoubtedly a valuable source of additional information, but it is important to be aware of their limitations. The surveys consist of interviews conducted with a sample of the adult, household population. As a result, the information collected does not record crimes committed against public bodies, those not resident in households, and those under the age of 16. Also, the information collected is affected by the accuracy of the memory of the individuals interviewed and their willingness to take part. Technical issues concerned with the representativeness of the sample can also affect the results, although measures are taken to control this. The importance of this is that, while, as was said, these surveys have, without question, considerably extended our knowledge of the distribution of crime, they ought not to be seen as providing a complete or comprehensive source from which to describe the 'true' extent of crime in society.

The 1993 Scottish Crime Survey (SCS)

One use to which the results of crime surveys can be put is to extend the 'map' of trends in crime as it is drawn from the statistics recorded by the police. This can be done by comparing the trends as they are described by the recorded statistics with the trends as they are described by the survey. Such comparisons both give a fuller picture of the terrain and to some extent act also as a 'check' on the accuracy of the view obtained by using only police-recorded crime statistics. It is possible to do this for Scotland, for example, by using the recently published first results of the 1993 Scottish Crime Survey (all figures in this section are taken from Anderson and Leitch, 1994).

There are some limitations to these comparisons. First, they can only be made for the period from 1981–92 and not, for example, for the longer period from 1950. Second, direct comparisons can only be made between the two types of data for certain specific crimes and offences. These are vandalism, housebreaking, theft of a motor vehicle, theft of a bicycle, robbery and assault.

Nevertheless, the first comparison that it is useful to make is between the total number of incidents reported in the SCS and the proportion of these that are estimated to have been recorded by the police. On the basis of the 1993 survey, it has been estimated that only 39 per cent of incidents reported to the survey interviewers were recorded by the police. The ratio of unrecorded crime, as estimated from the surveys, to crimes recorded by the police has, however, fallen since 1981. This means that the dark figure of crime has reduced in size from 1981 to 1992, and the reason for this is that the rate of reporting crimes by the public appears to have risen. In 1981, 38 per cent of those who were victims of crime reported this to the police, compared to 51 per cent in 1992. The crimes most likely to be reported are theft of a motor vehicle (98 per cent), housebreaking (78 per cent) and robbery (68 per cent). Crimes such as vandalism were the least likely to be reported, and the reason given for this was that the incident was too trivial.

Since 1981, the police statistics have shown overall a rise in recorded crimes and offences in Scotland. The picture as described from the data collected by the surveys is more complex. The total number of comparable crimes recorded by the police rose by 52 per cent between 1981 and 1992, compared to just a 5 per cent rise in the figures from the SCS. If, however, a more detailed comparison is made with the SCS incidents that were reported to the police, a markedly different picture emerges as there has been a 45 per cent rise in such incidents between 1981 and 1992, a figure much closer to the rate of increase as described by the police statistics.

A series of yet more detailed comparisons can be made between changes in the rate of increase in some of the types of crime mentioned earlier. First, if housebreaking, theft of a motor vehicle and bicycle theft are grouped together and their rate of increase is compared to that in the same grouping in the police statistics, then the rates of increase as described by the two sets of data are broadly the same. In the case of violent crimes (petty and serious assault and robbery), the comparison shows that there has been a decrease in the rate of the survey incidents, particularly since 1987, and an increase in these crimes over the same period as recorded in the police statistics. The comparative figures for vandalism show that, whereas in the police statistics this crime is recorded as having increased, in the survey the opposite holds true, where a decrease in incidents is reported.

These brief comparisons between the statistics recorded by the police and those generated by the crime survey show this to be a complex topic in which any conclusion drawn must be qualified and regarded as provisional. Some general, tentative statements can, however, be made. For the period in which comparisons can be made, and for those crimes and offences which can be compared, it appears that the increase described in police-recorded crime statistics has not been matched by a corresponding increase as described by the crime surveys. The reason why the rate of increase as described in the police-recorded statistics is so much greater is that there appears to have been an increase in the public's willingness to report crimes to the police. This would account for the general upward trend in the police statistics compared to the much flatter one for the rate of increase in the survey incidents.

Comparisons with England and Wales

The evidence from crime surveys allows comparisons in patterns of victimisation to be made between Scotland on the one hand and England and Wales on the other for the 1980s. In 1981, the rates of victimisation north and south of the border were similar, but by 1987, differences had begun to develop, with Scotland showing lower rates of victimisation for most types of crime; and these differences have continued to widen. For example, comparing the SCS (1993) with the British Crime Survey (1991), the figures for rates of victimisation for housebreaking are 607 per 10,000 households for Scotland, compared to 678 per 10,000 households for England and Wales; for all vehicle thefts, the comparative figures are 1,188 per 10,000 and 1,890 per 10,000; and for vandalism 1,048 per 10,000 compared to 1,357. In the areas of thefts from the person, assault and robbery, the differences are greater (measured per 10,000 individuals over the age of 16). The comparative figures for thefts from the person are 50 in Scotland and 108 in England and Wales; for assault, 380 compared to 586; and for robbery, 31 compared to 45.

These comparisons have to be set in the broader context of known differences in the comparative rate of public reporting of incidents to the police. The surveys show that in Scotland a higher percentage of survey incidents are reported to the police than in England and Wales. For example, in 1981, in Scotland, 38 per cent of survey incidents were reported to the police, compared to 35 per cent in England and Wales. By 1992, the figure for Scotland was 52 per cent and that for England and Wales (1991) was 44 per cent.

It is not clear why these differences exist but it does appear reasonable to conclude that there probably are differences in the rates of victimisation and, by inference, crime between Scotland and England and Wales, with the rates for Scotland being noticeably lower.

Conclusion

This chapter has discussed a number of problems concerned with the use of the official statistics on crime and has also provided brief descriptions of the major trends in crimes and offences in Scotland for the period between 1950 and 1994. As it stands, the chapter does little more than scratch the surface of a very complex field of enquiry. There are some very general conclusions that can be drawn, both about trends in crimes and offences and about the use of the various types of data we possess. It does appear that crime is increasing in Scotland but at a slower rate than in England and Wales. A great deal of crime is connected, directly and indirectly, with motor vehicles and with crimes of dishonesty relating to property. The more serious crimes, such as those involving violence and indecency, are significantly less common than those of dishonesty or those involving motor vehicles.

Chapter 3

———————◆———————

THE CRIMINAL JUSTICE SYSTEM AS A PROCESS

The main purpose of this chapter and those that follow is to examine the way in which the criminal justice system in Scotland responds to the crimes and offences described in Chapter 2. The main focus will be on young and adult offenders: young offenders are defined as those aged 16 but below 21; adult offenders are defined as those aged 21 or above. Scotland has a unique juvenile justice system called the Children's Hearings system, or the Children's Panel, which caters for those under 16 (up to 18 if they are already under the supervision of the system), and a separate chapter is devoted later to this system.

The specific objective of this chapter is to provide an overview of the criminal justice system in Scotland, to make the reader familiar with the names of the various institutions involved but also to introduce a particular conception of how the system may be described. This is the conception of the system as a process.

Criminal Justice as a Process

There are a number of reasons why criminologists use the concept of 'process' to describe the way in which the criminal justice system works. The main one is dissatisfaction with the use of the concept of 'system' as an accurate description of the manner in which the various institutions which deal with crime are related to one another. The idea of a 'system' can be seen to create the impression that there exists a streamlined, tight-knit organisation, whose parts are related by a grand design which, itself, has a clear purpose or purposes. There now exists a large body of research on the workings of criminal justice that casts doubt on whether the term 'system' adequately captures the very complex ways in which crime is handled. Rather, the image created by this research is of a number of separate organisations, such as the police, the criminal courts or the penal establishments, which are loosely related to one another. The research also suggests that these institutions do not always share the same view of matters but, rather, that there are a number of overlapping perspectives which may come into conflict. As with all institutions, there is also a competition for scarce resources.

Although this research refers to other countries, there is no reason to believe that it cannot be applied in a Scottish context. While, in comparative terms, the Scottish system is not large, it has to undertake more or less the same range of diverse and complex tasks. A 'modern' criminal justice system has to discharge many tasks and obligations, each of which has its unique features. For example, the jobs of the police and the courts do overlap but are also different; yet again, the work of a social worker is not the same as the police or as that of a prison officer or governor. The only real links between all these are that they are all concerned, in aspects of their work, with crime and criminals and that the criminal law forms one of the contexts in which they operate.

The Scottish Criminal Process

The flow chart presented in Figure 3.1 is taken from the 1994 statistical bulletin called *Criminal Proceedings in Scottish Criminal Courts*. This is a bulletin which is published annually and mostly describes the ways in which the criminal courts deal with crime; it also, usefully, describes the other possible courses of action that can be followed in the criminal process.

35

Figure 3.1 Overview of action within the criminal justice process, 1994.

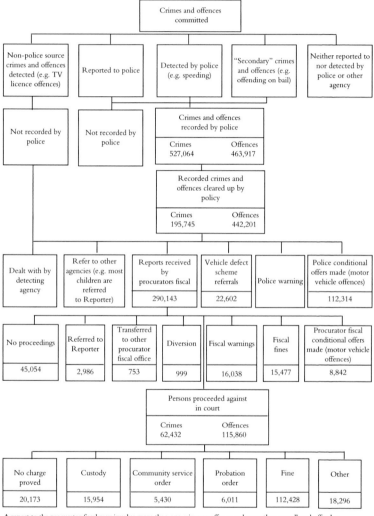

A report to the procurator fiscal may involve more than one crime or offence and more than one alleged offender.

The total number of reports to the fiscal includes reports on non-criminal matters such as sudden deaths. Fiscal outcomes are final outcomes and do not, for example, include reports initially marked for fiscal fines which were not accepted and where the fiscal took no further proceedings. In 1994, 20,000 reports received by the fiscal resulted in no further proceedings.

Figures for persons proceeded against count the number of occasions on which a person is proceeded against, not the number of crimes or offences involved.

A number of outcomes may result in subsequent prosecutions or referrals to other agencies, for example if a condition such as the payment of a fixed penalty is not complied with. For simplicity, these pathways are not shown in the diagram.

Crimes recorded in 1994 may not be cleared up or dealt with until 1995 or later.

Source: Criminal Proceedings in Scottish Courts.

There are several important lessons that can be learnt from studying Figure 3.1. It shows the number of separate decisions that must be taken by different organisations and individuals to process cases, from the stage of reporting or detection, through the stage of deciding on prosecution, to the criminal court, and then, finally, describes the range of available sanctions. The figure makes clear the complexity of decision-making involved and highlights also the various alternatives that are possible at each stage. For example, the diagram lists five possible different courses of action before an incident ends up being recorded by the police and entered into the recorded crime statistics. It shows that only three of them will lead to an event being recorded. The figure also illustrates the range of options open to the police once they have cleared up a crime, only one of which involves a report to the procurator fiscal.

In many ways, the most complex stage is that which comes after a report to the procurator fiscal, when the range of possible courses of action expands yet further. As is clear from the flow chart, the procurator fiscal has a number of options, only one of which is to go ahead with a prosecution in the criminal courts. Many cases are dealt with without going to court, either by a decision not to proceed at all, or by the fiscal dealing with the case and thus halting the process at this stage. A subsequent chapter will describe in more detail what is involved in decision-making at this crucial juncture. It may be helpful to point out, however, that a precondition of the fiscal issuing a warning or diverting a case in any way is that a prior decision must have been reached that a prosecution would be possible. The decision to deal with a case in any of the alternatives portrayed must, therefore, be a positive one.

This leads naturally on to the next stage in the criminal justice process – a case being heard in the criminal court. Again the flow chart shows the various alternatives available. A good number of cases end with there being no charge proved, which means that a verdict of not guilty or not proven has been reached or that, for some other reason, the charge has not been established. If the verdict is one of guilty, then a number of options are possible. Thereafter, the case enters the penal system, the primary task of which is to administer the punishment determined by the court.

This brief account of the passage of cases through the criminal justice process shows several things. First, it should help to illustrate the number of decisions that have to be made before a case ends up in a criminal court. At each stage in the proceedings, at least one decision has to be made before the case can go any further. The criminal justice system ought not to be seen as a mechanical system in which a case proceeds through a series of inevitable stages; rather, the flow chart shows its complex and fluid nature.

Second, the account helps to bring out another important theme: that the criminal justice process is selective. This can be seen by noting the number of cases that are eliminated at each stage. It is difficult, however, to calculate in precise quantitative terms how many cases 'disappear' between the early and late stages of the process because the unit of counting changes. In the chart, this occurs at the stage of the police reporting to the procurator fiscal and also then at the court stage where the unit counted shifts to persons proceeded against. As the notes at the bottom of the chart make clear, in both cases, more than one crime or offence may be involved in these units. For example, a report made to the fiscal may contain information on a number of crimes or offences. By contrast, at the stage of the police, each crime or offence is recorded separately. While these changes in the unit of counting may rule out strict calculations of 'flows' throughout the system, it is still, nevertheless, possible to present precise figures within each stage and beyond to build up a more impressionistic overview of the selective nature of the process as a whole.

One interesting general observation which can be made is that, as the flow chart shows, more crimes than offences 'leave' the criminal process at the police stage. This is shown, in the chart, by the higher clear-up rate for offences as compared to crimes. As the chart shows, the police recorded 527,064 crimes and 463,917 offences in 1994. Only 195,745 crimes, however, were recorded as cleared up compared to 442,201 offences. There are, of course, many reasons why more offences than crimes are cleared up, perhaps the main one being that the police themselves 'discover' more recorded offences in circumstances which lead them automatically to a suspect, whereas they are much more reliant on the public for information about crimes without necessarily receiving information about a suspect.

At the later stages of the process, the reverse seems to hold; that is, crimes appear to stay in the process for longer and thus are more likely to end up being prosecuted in the courts. It can be seen from the chart that the procurator fiscal and the police divert more offences than crimes. In 1994, for instance, 121,156 offences were diverted to a conditional offer. This, of course, is to be expected on the grounds that the more serious crimes ought to be pursued in the court. Nevertheless, some crimes do leave the process before reaching the courts, for example by no further proceedings taking place (45,054 cases in 1994).

Again, there are many reasons why crimes which are cleared up by the police leave the criminal justice process. For example, the fact that the police report a crime to the prosecutor does not in itself mean that a prosecution is justified. As is explained in more detail in the next chapter, the procurator fiscal has to consider a number of factors before deciding that a prosecution is justified in a particular case, including whether there is sufficient evidence and if it is in the public interest to prosecute. If the fiscal should decide on either or both grounds that a prosecution is not justified, then the case will leave the system at this point.

The selective nature of the system can be captured by the use of metaphors or similes. The criminal process is said to be a filter or, rather, a series of filters, each of which has a different mesh. Or, alternatively, the process may be likened to a series of gates, each of which needs to be opened before a case can pass through; at each stage there are gatekeepers who can decide what to let through and what to stop. In the context of the criminal justice process, the principal gatekeepers are the police and the procurator fiscal, and it is they, among others, who control exits and entrances.

The Process in Criminal Cases

The purpose of this brief section is to provide a more detailed outline of the procedures through which a case may pass on its journey from the reporting of the crime or offence to the disposal of the perpetrator by a criminal court. These procedures are of interest for a number of reasons. First, Figures 3.2 and 3.3 show the complexity of the process; cases do not simply pass from apprehension by the police directly to the court, but will go through various intermediate stages of examination. The diagrams also help to illustrate the mixed nature of the Scottish criminal justice process mentioned in Chapter 1. Scottish criminal procedure at the pre-trial stage is, in some respects, inquisitorial. There are various forms of pre-trial examination of the accused, aimed at fact-gathering, often with the purpose of minimising delays by introducing a greater certainty into the proceedings. At the point of trial, however, the process is clearly adversarial (see page 87 for a fuller discussion of the distinction between adversarial and inquisitorial procedure).

Figure 3.2   Stages in summary procedure.

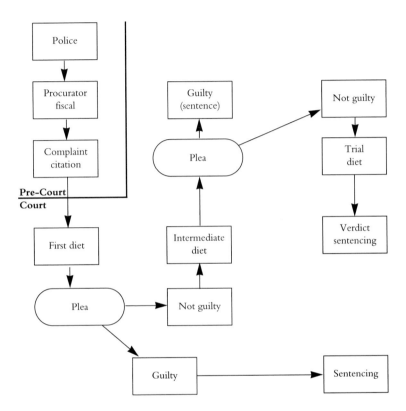

The purpose of Figures 3.2 and 3.3 is to show the main stages in the progress of a case. More detail of what happens at each stage is contained in the subsequent chapters. The exact procedures followed depend on a primary decision taken by the public prosecutor. Serious crimes are usually dealt with by solemn procedure, while the less serious crimes and the offences are dealt with by summary procedure. The essential difference between the two is that in summary procedure the judge decides the case without a jury even if there is a plea of not guilty. In solemn procedure a plea of not guilty is decided before a jury. In both

Figure 3.3   Stages in solemn procedure.

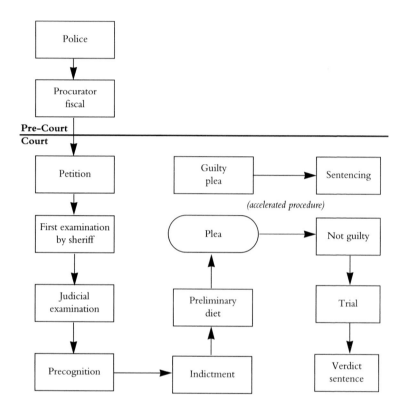

procedures there will normally be a defence agent and a prosecutor present. Historically, summary procedure evolved as a quicker way of disposing of cases of a less serious nature. As will be seen in Chapter 6, the vast majority of cases in Scotland are dealt with by summary procedure.

Figures 3.2 and 3.3 present a picture of all the stages a case could pass through. Before describing what happens at each of the stages portrayed, there are two general points to be made.

First, in the last few years the government has engaged in a wide-ranging review of many aspects of these procedures in criminal cases. The aim of this review is to bring about improvements in the delivery of justice in Scotland. As part of this review process, the government issued a number of consultation papers on many aspects of the criminal process, including evidence and procedure, legal aid, juries and verdicts, sentencing and appeals, and the right to silence, judicial examination and evidence of previous convictions. A White Paper, *Firm and Fair* (1996), containing the results of most of these consultations and announcing plans for legislation, was published in June 1994. This has been followed by a major Criminal Justice Act, the Criminal Justice (Scotland) Act 1995 which received Royal Assent in the summer of 1995.

The second general point is that while Figures 3.2 and 3.3 provide a full picture of the stages that may be passed through, it does not follow that every case will pass through all of them. There are, for example, ways of accelerating cases in solemn procedure. It is possible for the accused to intimate to the procurator fiscal an intention to plead guilty, and if this is accepted an 'accelerated' procedure is followed. The case appears before the court, and sentence can be passed.

As Figures 3.2 and 3.3 show, every case is considered by the procurator fiscal, who makes many crucial decisions. Most reports about crime are made by the police, but many other agencies also report crimes and offences to the procurator fiscal (see Chapter 4). Once the prosecutor has decided (1) to prosecute and (2) under what procedure, the courses to be followed are quite different.

Summary Procedure

Summary procedure is governed by the Criminal Procedure (Scotland) Act 1995. Summary procedure is confined to the sheriff and the district courts, the composition and powers of which are described in Chapter 6.

If the fiscal decides to prosecute, the charge for the alleged offence is set out in a complaint. The complaint also specifies the court in which the case will be heard. A complaint, however, is only one way of bringing the accused to court. Where an accused has been released on an undertaking to appear, he will be served with a complaint and a citation.

The First Diet

The first diet is the first calling of the accused to court, although the accused need not attend in person. The accused will normally be represented by a solicitor of his or her own choosing or by the duty solicitor provided under the legal aid scheme (see Chapter 6). The purpose of the first diet is to establish a plea, although the accused need not enter a plea at this stage. Questions to the relevancey of the complaint, or a denial that the accused is the person charged by the police, will normally be settled at this stage.

If the accused pleads guilty, the court can move to sentence or, if it wishes, to obtain reports on the offender, adjourn matters and set a date for sentence to be passed.

If there is no plea or a plea of not guilty, then a date will be set for a trial.

The Intermediate Diet

The court, or either the prosecution or the defence, may call for an intermediate diet to be held. The purpose of an intermediate diet is to find out how well prepared the prosecution and the accused are with the case and to see if the accused wishes to persist with a plea of not guilty. The accused must attend an intermediate diet.

The intermediate diet was introduced in 1980 to try and reduce the number of cases in which pleas of guilty were put forward on the day of the trial as it was thought that this quite common practice caused considerable inconvenience to all involved. Last-minute changes of plea are still very common. The Criminal Justice (Scotland) Act 1995 requires an intermediate diet in all summary cases prosecuted in the sheriff courts and the district courts. The Act sets out the purposes of the intermediate diet which are said to be (1) to ascertain whether the prosecution and defence cases are fully prepared, (2) to ascertain whether the Crown and defence are in a position to agree any evidence so that, where appropriate, witnesses can be discharged, (3) to enquire if a joint minute of agreement or statement of facts is agreed, and (4) if the cases are not fully prepared or the above agreements cannot be reached, to set a new trial diet or to continue the intermediate diet on another date.

The purpose of these measures is to make sure that more cases go to trial on time. It is thought that in the past too many cases did not go to trial on schedule with a resulting 'waste' of time for the witness involved and for the court. The mandatory use of intermediate diets is aimed at keeping such delays to a minimum. An accused may plead guilty at an intermediate diet, and, if this happens, matters proceed as described above.

The Criminal Justice (Scotland) Act 1995 also contains a number of other measures aimed at making the trial process more efficient, without reducing the rights of the accused. For example, the prosecution and defence are required to take all reasonable steps to secure agreement on matters which might be agreed or admitted without a challenge. This measure is aimed at requiring both sides to do all that is possible to decide what evidence is to be contested and what will be uncontested. In the case of the latter, there will be a duty to agree this evidence and to make this clear to the court at the intermediate diet.

Trial Diet

The trial diet is the occasion on which a verdict will normally be reached. The trial diet can be postponed or abandoned. If the accused fails to appear, the normal proceeding is for the prosecutor to move for a warrant for the arrest of the person. It is possible, however, for the trial to proceed in the absence of the accused if the charge is one for a statutory offence which does not merit imprisonment.

The accused will normally be represented by a solicitor who may be the one who was earlier provided under the legal aid scheme. The accused may, however, choose to retain his or her own solicitor and, if further legal aid has been refused, the expense of this must be borne by the accused.

Solemn Procedure

Solemn procedure is the name given to the means by which the more serious crimes are handled. If the case goes to trial with a plea of not guilty, it will be decided before a jury of 15 members of the public who have been selected to sit on the case. Solemn procedure is also known as 'petition procedure' or 'procedure on indictment'. These names are used because the initiating writ is known as a petition and the indictment is the document in which the charge against the accused is specified. Solemn procedure is confined to the sheriff and the High Court (see Chapter 6). The law governing solemn procedure is set out in the Criminal Procedure (Scotland) Act 1995. The various stages through which a case may pass are portrayed in Figure 3.3.

Petition and First Examination

The charge in a case brought under solemn procedure is nearly always first set out in a petition issued by the procurator fiscal.

The accused will first appear before a sheriff even if the final destination of the case is the High Court. This appearance is known as 'first examination' and is held in private; any additional appearances are known as 'further examination'.

The accused is entitled to make a declaration at the first examination but is not required to do so. The declaration is a verbal statement, in the accused's own words, containing anything he or she wishes to say about the crime with which they have been charged. The declaration is not a plea, although, of course, it may well contain statements which, in effect, admit or deny the charge. The accused is entitled to the advice of a solicitor before making a declaration. This solicitor will be provided free under the legal aid scheme until the accused is either released on bail or fully committed, or until an application to the court for further legal aid is granted or denied. The accused can choose to have his or her own solicitor present.

In most cases the first examination is formal and brief, with the accused's solicitor informing the court that the accused does not wish to make any statement. The fiscal then proceeds to ask the court that the accused be committed for trial or for further examination.

Judicial Examination

A judicial examination is a further appearance before a sheriff, called on the instigation of the fiscal. The purpose of a judicial examination is for the prosecution to try and clarify any statements made by the accused to the police and to establish if any special defence is likely to be led. The prosecution is not allowed to cross-examine the accused or to challenge the truth of any statement made by the accused. The accused is not on oath and the task of the sheriff is to ensure that the questions are put fairly by the prosecutor and that the accused understands the questions.

The accused is permitted to have a solicitor present and may consult the solicitor before answering any question. The accused is not obliged to answer questions put by the prosecutor. There is restricted scope for the solicitor to ask questions if granted permission by the sheriff. The questions must be aimed at clarifying any ambiguities arising from answers given by the accused. It is proposed that if the accused exercises the right to silence at this stage then it may be mentioned at a later date in the trial and inferences drawn from it. The proceedings of a judicial examination have to be taken down verbatim by a writer supplied by the fiscal, and a copy of the proceedings must be supplied to the accused and the solicitor.

Precognition

Once the accused is fully committed for trial the fiscal must have the case 'precognosed' in order that the Crown Counsel (see Chapter 5) may decide what proceedings to take (if any).

A precognition is a statement taken from a witness in which the witness says what he or she knows of the facts of the case. Precognitions may be taken under oath but this is not a requirement. After the fiscal has taken all precognitions, they are sent to the Crown Counsel who decide how the case should be dealt with. This can include taking no further action or dealing with the case on summary procedure.

If it is decided to deal with the case in the High Court, the Crown Counsel will prepare the indictment; if the case is to be dealt with in the sheriff court, the procurator fiscal will prepare the indictment.

The Indictment

This is the document which contains details of the charge against the accused and is presented in the name of the Lord Advocate (see Chapter 5).

It is only with the serving of the indictment that the accused is officially informed of the charges against him or her and of the list of witnesses to be called and other evidence presented. The defence can then proceed to precognose witnesses.

Preliminary Diet

A preliminary diet is called if the accused wishes to challenge the competencey and relevancey of the indictment or part of it. Notice calling for a preliminary hearing must be lodged within fifteen days after being served with the indictment. The Criminal Justice (Scotland) Act 1995 has made preliminary diets mandatory in cases taken on solemn procedure in the sheriff court. The reasons for this as well as its purpose are the same as those that lie behind the introduction of mandatory intermediate diets in summary procedure. The statutory requirement for prosecution and defence to agree uncontested evidence before trial will apply in solemn procedure.

Accelerated Procedure

It is possible for the accused to inform the public prosecutor by letter of an intention to plead guilty. If this is accepted, then an accelerated procedure can be followed which will obviate the need for a trial diet.

Trial Diet

A plea of not guilty will be decided before a jury. As was indicated earlier, a jury is composed of fifteen members of the public who have not been barred from jury service by, for example, having served a prison sentence of three months or more and who have not been rehabilitated under the

Rehabilitation of Offenders Act 1974. A person who has been sentenced to a period of imprisonment of five years or more is permanently barred from jury service. There are also a number of individuals who are ineligible by their profession from serving on a jury, such as those involved in the administration of justice. Members of either House of Parliament and members of the armed services and the medical profession are eligible for jury service but have a right to be excused.

The jury is selected by the prosecution and the defence from those called to court. It was possible, until the Criminal Justice (Scotland) Act 1995, for the prosecution or the defence to apply to have a single-sex jury or for the judge to decide to have one.

Once the jury has been selected and sworn in, the trial begins. There is an introduction by the judge but no opening speeches by the prosecution or the defence. The judge will introduce those appearing and briefly describe the procedures to be followed. The evidence by the Crown is led first.

After both sides have presented their cases and made any other submissions, the judge will 'charge' the jury. This means the judge will tell the jury what the law is which applies to the case. There is no duty for the judge to sum up the evidence. The judge will inform the jury that the onus of the proof is on the Crown and advise that the standard of proof is one beyond all reasonable doubt. All evidence in criminal cases has to be corroborated, which means that there must be two independent sources to confirm the evidence that the two sides wish to lead. An accused cannot be convicted on his or her confession alone, unless the evidence contained in the confession is that which could only be known by the perpetrator of the crime with which the accused has been charged.

The jury will then be secluded to reach its decision. In Scotland a simple majority decision has long been permissible. The expression is that a decision may be reached by 'not less than eight' members of the jury. There are three verdicts possible: guilty, not guilty, and not proven. The last verdict is unique to Scotland and has the same effect as a finding of not guilty. The accused can walk free and no further charges relating to the crime with which the accused was charged may be brought at a later date (for a fuller discussion of verdicts see Chapter 6).

Conclusion

This chapter has tried to suggest a useful perspective – that of process – as a way of understanding the operation of criminal justice in Scotland. A description has also been given of the various procedural stages a case may pass through on its route through the criminal courts. The subsequent chapters will build upon these foundations by looking at the criminal process in three stages: first, the pre-court or, more precisely, the pre-prosecution stage up to and including the role of the public prosecutor; second, the court stage; third, beyond the criminal justice process into the penal system.

Chapter 4

◆

THE PROCESSING OF CRIME:
THE POLICE AND THE PROCURATOR FISCAL

The purpose of this chapter is to provide an overview of the police and the public prosecution services in Scotland. As we saw in Chapter 3, both these institutions occupy a key place in the criminal justice process; they act as gatekeepers to the rest of the criminal process by controlling many of the cases that enter and flow through it. An understanding of how they are organised, of the nature of their powers and of their work is, therefore, crucial.

The Police: The Political and Organisational Context

Scotland does not have a single or national police force. Rather, the organisation of the police reflects a balance between the power of local and central government and the position of Chief Constables, who possess considerable independence in operational matters.

There are eight police forces in Scotland: Central, Dumfries and Galloway, Fife, Grampian, Lothian and Borders, Northern, Strathclyde, and Tayside. These forces were created in 1975 as part of the major reorganisation of local government which took place that year. Before 1975, there were 22 police forces and, immediately after the Second World War, there were 49. The largest police force is Strathclyde, which is responsible for policing just under half of the population in Scotland and has over half the total number of police officers in the country.

Each police force is maintained by a police authority or joint board composed of elected local authority councillors. The police authority determines the budget for the force and provides the resources necessary for effective policing of the area; the authority is also responsible for appointing senior officers and for deciding on the number of officers and civilians employed. Police forces are jointly financed by local and central government. The Secretary of State has powers to control the pay and allowances of the police and can issue guidance to police authorities and to Chief Constables on a wide range of policing matters. The Secretary of State has to approve the appointment of senior officers of the rank of Assistant Chief Constable and above.

While each force is under the control of the local authority and the Secretary of State in matters of broad policy, it is the Chief Constable who is responsible for day-to-day police operations, the deployment of the force, and the enforcement of law within the force area. The Chief Constable cannot be directed in these matters by either the Secretary of State or the police authority. The Chief Constable does, however, have a duty to comply with instructions from the Lord Advocate, other relevant procurators fiscal and the Sheriff Principal, but is otherwise independent and responsible for the efficient and effective use of the resources provided by the police authority. Chief Constables have to prepare an annual report which must be submitted to the police authority and copied to the Secretary of State and to the local Sheriff Principal. Her Majesty's Inspectors of Constabulary, on the direction of the Secretary of State, can visit forces and enquire into their efficiency; their reports are submitted to the Secretary of State.

The Internal Structure of Police Forces

Police forces undertake a wide range of functions, from traditional uniformed officers engaged in general policing, patrolling the streets, preventing crime, preserving the peace and responding to and assisting the public, to more specialist tasks including criminal investigation and traffic management. Additional support is also provided by specialist services such as forensic science units and computer and communications services which involve an extensive use of information technology. A very important aspect of the responsibilities of a contemporary police force is the emphasis placed upon liaison with and support of the community. The latter involves a special responsibility for juveniles and for crime prevention. The general area of crime prevention is accorded a high priority by police forces, who work with local community groups, voluntary organisations and local industry and local authorities as well as other criminal justice agencies to promote effective crime prevention strategies. There is also a Scottish Crime Prevention Council and a Crime Prevention Unit. The national policy on crime prevention is set out in *Preventing Crime Together in Scotland: A Strategy for the 90s*, published in 1992.

The ranks within the police are common to all branches: constable, sergeant, inspector, chief inspector, superintendent, assistant Chief Constable and Chief Constable.

In 1992, there were 14,094 police officers in Scotland, as compared to 13,518 in 1988. The police service remains male-dominated: in 1990, women officers constituted 9 per cent of the total force. In an attempt to increase this percentage, efforts have been made recently to recruit more females.

Police Duties and Powers

The Police (Scotland) Act 1967 (as amended by subsequent legislation) specifies the organisational structure of the police forces in Scotland, including the general duties of Chief Constables. The police have a general duty to uphold and enforce the law and also to maintain peace. In order to exercise these duties the police have certain powers to arrest and to detain individuals who are suspected of committing criminal acts or who are caught in the process of doing so. These are important powers not least because they can infringe on the liberty of the citizen. These powers are partly the result of common law provision and are also set out in a number of statutes, the most general and recent of which is the Criminal Justice (Scotland) Act 1980. The purpose of the common law and the statutory framework is both to invest the police with certain powers and also to put limits on their exercise.

It is important to state, because they are often confused or seen to be the same, that arrest and detention are distinct. For example, an individual can, under certain circumstances, be detained in a police station without being arrested.

Arrest

The police may arrest a suspect either with or without a warrant. A warrant is a written authority that gives the police the power to arrest a named person and it may include also the authority to search a specified place. The warrant can be issued by a judge of any court or a justice of the peace and is granted only after information is provided by the procurator fiscal or by the sworn testimony of a police officer, a customs officer, a social worker or other persons. A warrant should be executed as soon as possible. When a person is arrested on a warrant, the warrant should be shown to the arrestee if he or she asks to look at it. If a warrant is in existence, but there is no fear that the person named will abscond, then it is not necessary for that person to be taken into custody. Rather, the person should be told that the warrant is in existence and then be invited to attend at a certain time and place; such attendance is equivalent to the execution of the warrant as is required by consideration of the various time limits on prosecution.

Although there is a general preference in Scots law for arrest to be made on the basis of a warrant whenever this is possible, there are times when this is impractical (for example, arrest to stop a suspect leaving the scene of a crime) or when it may be unnecessary (in the case of minor crimes). In these and certain other circumstances, the police may arrest without a warrant.

The power to arrest a suspect without a warrant is, however, a complex and delicate issue. It is regulated by common law but it is recognised that it is difficult to state this law clearly. This is because the propriety of an arrest always depends on the circumstances in which the arrest was made. It is further complicated because there is no distinction in Scots criminal law between arrestable and non-arrestable crimes and offences. Rather, all crimes and offences are regarded as breaches of the peace and thereby potentially arrestable with or without warrant.

There are, however, a number of general common law principles governing arrest without warrant that have emerged over time. The most general of these is that an arrest is justified only if it can be seen that, at the time, it was reasonable for the constable to have believed that it was in the interests of justice to carry out the arrest. This belief can, of course, be challenged and, if the challenge proves successful, the arrest will have been shown to have been unlawful. It does not follow, however, that either a subsequent conviction or discharge would in themselves demonstrate the propriety or impropriety of the arrest. The reasonableness of the constable's action will be judged according to such factors as the arrestee's character, whether the person arrested has a 'fixed abode', and considerations of the seriousness of the crime – murder may in itself, for example, be seen to justify an arrest. Moreover, the courts have held that the arrest of a 'known criminal' is easier to justify than that of a 'law-abiding', 'respectable' householder.

These examples show that arrest without a warrant is justified if it can be shown that, on challenge, the constable exercised the use of his or her discretion reasonably in the pursuit of the general objective of upholding the ends of justice. Beyond consideration of these general principles it is difficult to specify in any detail the circumstances in which an arrest without warrant would be justifiable or not.

Notwithstanding the open-ended nature of the common law powers of arrest, it is possible to describe certain typical circumstances in which an arrest without warrant would be justified. These include:

1. arresting a person who is committing, or attempting to commit, a serious crime;

2. arresting a person in possession of goods which the police officer believes to be stolen and the person being unable to account for them in a way which is consistent with innocence;

3. arresting a person who is committing a breach of the peace;

4. arresting a person after receiving information from a credible witness that the person has committed or is committing a crime.

The power to arrest without warrant in statutory offences can be conferred by the relevant statute or, again, be a matter of those powers the police possess in the common law. Where a statute gives a more limited power of arrest than would be available in the common law, any arrest must comply with the statute.

The more common statutory provisions for arrest without warrant are the Road Traffic Act 1988, the Prevention of Crime Act 1953, the Firearms Act 1968 and the Misuse of Drugs Act

1971. The police also commonly carry out arrests without warrant in some statutory offences where the statute contains no provision for them to do so. Two examples which are important and relevant are the Police (Scotland) Act 1967 and the Sexual Offences (Scotland) Act 1976.

Detention

Until the coming into force of sections 1 and 2 of the Criminal Justice (Scotland) Act 1980, the police had no power to take a person into custody unless that person was arrested. The 1980 Act (sections 1 and 2), however, changed this situation by conferring on the police the power to detain a person for limited periods without an arrest or a charge being made.

Section 1 regulates what is sometimes called 'on-street' detention, although it is not confined to streets. The section empowers the police to require a suspect to identify him- or herself, to provide an explanation of the circumstances which gave rise to the constable's suspicions, and to remain with the constable until the information so acquired is verified. The police are also given powers to use reasonable force to ensure that a suspect does indeed stay with the officer. These powers also apply to the detention of witnesses. If a person, without reasonable excuse, refuses to give the information requested, or to remain with the police officer, he or she will be guilty of an offence and liable, on conviction, to pay a fine.

While this section gives the police certain powers, it also stipulates certain conditions that affect their exercise. These conditions oblige the officer to explain to the detainee the grounds of suspicion, the general nature of the offence that the officer believes the person to have committed or to be in the process of committing, and why the person is being required to remain with the officer.

Section 2 of the Act gives the police power to detain a suspect in a police station for the purposes of investigation. For these powers to be used, the officer must suspect the person of committing or having committed an offence punishable by imprisonment.

This section gives the police the power to detain such an individual for up to six hours. The detention is terminated by the person being arrested and charged or by there no longer being any suspicions of the sort referred to above. If a person is detained for six hours he or she must be informed of the time at which the detention began and when the six hours have expired; both times must be recorded by a police officer.

The section describes a number of safeguards similar to those which are outlined in Section 1 of the Act. The person who is detained must be informed of the general nature of the offence which he or she is suspected of committing or of having committed and of the grounds of the officer's suspicions. The person must be informed that he or she is under no obligation to answer any question other than to give his or her name and address. The person has the right to inform a solicitor as was described above. The time at which such contact is made must also be recorded.

As was said, the purpose of this section of the Act is to give the police the power to detain a person for investigation, including questioning. The police have the power to take fingerprints and any such other prints and impressions as the constable considers appropriate in the circumstances of the suspected offence. The police are empowered to use reasonable force to achieve these ends.

Search

A person may be searched with or without a warrant. Generally speaking, however, a person may not be searched, nor may premises be searched, unless a court has granted a warrant.

Search without a Warrant

At common law, a search of a person or premises without a warrant is justifiable on the grounds of urgency. Also some statutes, such as the Misuse of Drugs Act 1971, the Criminal Justice (Scotland) Act 1980 and the Civic Government (Scotland) Act 1982, provide for searches of persons or premises without warrant, but require a police officer to have reasonable grounds for suspecting that a crime has been or is being committed before proceeding with the search.

Search with a Warrant

A search warrant may be granted by any magistrate, at common law. Some statutes require the magistrate to take evidence on oath before granting a warrant, such as the Misuse of Drugs Act 1971.

A warrant may be issued although no person has been charged or arrested, as all that is necessary is that the person applying for the warrant, for example the procurator fiscal, has reasonable grounds for suspecting that a crime has been committed. The application should name the crime and, if possible, the suspect.

Once a person has been committed for trial on solemn procedure or had a date fixed for trial under summary procedure, it is not normally possible for further searches of the person or premises to be made.

Procedure after Arrest

When a person is arrested and detained, he or she must be told immediately of the general nature of the charge on which the arrest was made. The person also has a right to be brought before a court as soon as possible. The Summary Jurisdiction (Scotland) Act 1954 requires that, wherever possible, a person shall be brought before a court not later than the first day after being taken into custody. A failure to comply with this does not, however, negate the validity of any subsequent prosecution. An arrested person may be detained in a police station or cell between arrest and appearance at court. The arrested person has a right to let his or her solicitor know of their arrest and to advice from the solicitor before the appearance in court; there is also an entitlement to let other individuals know that he or she has been arrested, unless this knowledge interferes with the ends of justice. An individual has a right to be told this information on arrival at a police station. Once a person has been arrested, he or she is protected from further police questioning on the charge for which the arrest took place.

The powers of the police to arrest and detain form what is perhaps the core legal context within which they conduct their work. These powers are enabling (in that they allow the police to do certain things) and also regulatory (as limits are put upon these powers and how they are to be exercised). It has long been recognised, however, that the law forms only one context among others which influence how the police perform their duties and conduct their work.

The nature of police work, including the examination of how they exercise their legal powers of arrest, detention and search, has been a topic which has attracted considerable attention from criminologists and other social scientists who have sought to investigate the issue by conducting various types of empirical inquiries.

Many of the investigations show how difficult a job policing is. It is impossible to go into these studies in any great depth here, not least because they are so numerous. They are relevant, however, as they cast light on the role of the police. Of particular interest is the description these studies give of what is called 'police occupational culture'. Research has shown that the police have evolved a culture which has an influence on how they perceive their role in society, their job and thus how they go about their work. It is said to be this occupational culture which forms a key context within which the police exercise the very considerable discretion that they possess at all levels of the organisation, including that of the ordinary police constable.

Clear-up Rates

One important measure of the efficiency of the police, which they take seriously themselves, is the extent to which they clear up crime. Clear-up rates, as they are known, have received attention recently as part of the government's general policy of endeavouring to ensure value for money in public services.

A crime is cleared up if one or more offenders are apprehended, cited, warned or traced for it. This definition of a 'clear-up' is broader than the simple idea that a conviction has been secured. On the basis of the official definition, the clear-up rate for 1982 for all recorded crimes (excluding offences) was 30 per cent, and this rose to 37 per cent by 1994. The number of crimes recorded per police officer rose over the period from 28 in 1980 to 37 in 1994, and the number of crimes cleared up per police officer increased from 9 in 1980 to 14 in 1994. The clear-up figure for recorded miscellaneous offences was 86 per cent in 1994; the number of such offences cleared up per police officer was 31 in 1994.

As can be seen, there is a substantial difference in the clear-up rate between crimes and offences, which largely reflects the way the police get to know of offences. In many cases the offender is caught in the act by the police, as, for example, in drunk driving and speeding offences.

There is a considerable variation in the clear-up rates between different crimes. The lower clear-up rate for crimes is largely the result of the low clear-up rate for the most frequently occurring types of crime. For example, the clear-up rate in 1994 for housebreaking was 17 per cent (19 per cent in 1980); for theft by opening a lockfast place it was 15 per cent (19 per cent in 1980); and for theft of motor vehicle 24 per cent (28 per cent in 1980). In 1994, the clear-up rate for sexual assault was 68 per cent, for serious assault 57 per cent, and for vandalism 20 per cent.

There is some variation in the clear-up rate between different police forces. Central Scotland police force has the highest recorded clear-up rate for recorded crimes (57 per cent) and Strathclyde and Grampian have the lowest (34 per cent) (1994 figures).

The System of Public Prosecution

As was stated in Chapter 1, the public prosecutor, particularly the procurator fiscal, plays a central role in the Scottish criminal justice system. The fiscal receives all police reports, makes the crucial decision in the vast majority of cases about whether to prosecute and then determines the venue and the type of procedure under which the prosecution will take place. In addition, as was seen in Chapter 3, the fiscal controls entry to the various diversion schemes now in operation and also possesses the power to dispose of the case by issuing a warning or offering a fixed penalty (the fiscal fine, as it is known). These are extensive responsibilities and wide powers, the exercise of which has profound implications for the system as a whole. The objective of the next section will be to describe the organisation of the system of public prosecution and to discuss the policy which guides it.

The Organisation of the Public Prosecution System

The head of the system of public prosecution in Scotland is the Lord Advocate. Besides these duties, the Lord Advocate is also the principal law officer of the Crown in Scotland and, as a member of the government of the day, a UK minister, who leaves office if the government is defeated. The Lord Advocate is also the government's chief constitutional and legal adviser on Scottish affairs.

The Lord Advocate's powers are discharged through a number of separate civil service departments. Those connected with prosecution are discharged through the Crown Office, which is located in Edinburgh, and serves as the administrative headquarters of the procurator fiscal service; its administrative head is the Crown Agent. The procurator fiscal service has a devolved responsibility for processing all criminal cases and for the actual prosecution of criminal cases in the sheriff and district courts throughout the country. The fiscal service also has a responsibility for the holding of fatal accident inquiries and for investigating complaints against the police. In total, the fiscal receives reports from approximately 50 different agencies, including Customs and Excise, the Health and Safety Executive and the social work departments of local authorities; all such reports have to be examined and the decision taken as to whether to prosecute. There is a procurator fiscal for each sheriffdom in Scotland and for each sheriff court district; at present there are 49 procurators fiscal in Scotland who are supported by a number of assistants of various grades (known as assistant or depute procurators fiscal). All procurators fiscal are qualified lawyers, usually solicitors; they are employed as civil servants.

Prosecution in the High Court of Justiciary is conducted for the Lord Advocate by Advocates Depute (of which there are 12), known, together with the Solicitor-General for Scotland, as Crown Counsel. Rights of audience have been extended to solicitor advocates, and consideration is being given to whether solicitor advocates in the procurator fiscal service, as well as those in private practice, might be appointed as Advocates Depute. The Solicitor-General is the other law officer for Scotland and, like the Lord Advocate, is a minister of the government. The Solicitor-General assists the Lord Advocate in the full range of his or her duties.

Procurators fiscal conduct the majority of prosecutions. Their role begins when they receive a report from the police or another one of the agencies mentioned above. The principal decision they take is whether to prosecute in a particular case. Generally, there are said to be two grounds on which prosecution decisions are made: whether there is enough evidence to justify a prosecution and whether it is in the public interest to do so.

In considering the first of these grounds, the fiscal will look at the strength of the available evidence and decide if it is sufficient to be likely to secure a conviction in the court. Even if there is enough evidence, however, the fiscal is not compelled by law to proceed with the prosecution. Rather, the fiscal may reach the decision that there are other, public interest, grounds that do not make it necessary or desirable to proceed. In Scotland, the primary emphasis has long been placed upon this criterion, and it is thus necessary to understand what is meant by the term.

The concept of the public interest in the context of prosecution can be interpreted in a number of ways. Traditionally, it has been understood to cover a variety of specific factors, such as the existence of special circumstances in the background or character of the accused or of the victim which may make prosecution inadvisable. Another set of grounds upon which a decision not to proceed to prosecution in the courts has traditionally been based is whether the information received has been inspired by malice on the part of the complainer, whether there are excusing or mitigating circumstances or whether the case is too trivial to warrant taking to court. Such circumstances have always been taken into account by the procurator fiscal in making decisions on prosecution and there is no reason to believe, or to wish, that this sort of discretion will not be exercised in the future.

Alternatives to Prosecution

More recently, however, the procurator fiscal has used his or her discretionary powers in a wider sense in deciding not to proceed to prosecution in certain cases. As a result, a policy of seeking alternatives to prosecution has developed which considerably extends the traditional use of discretion just described. The background to this development is the recommendations contained in the reports of the Thomson Committee and the Stewart Committee, which suggested that prosecution in the courts should be primarily reserved for the more serious crimes. The introduction in 1983 of the 'fixed-penalty' scheme for certain motor vehicle offences and the extension of the 'fiscal fine' to other minor offences in 1988 are two examples of how these recommendations have been put into practice. Under the fiscal fine scheme, for example, the fiscal makes a conditional offer to the accused of a fixed penalty as an alternative to prosecution in the court. Individuals can choose not to accept the offer and, in these circumstances, the case will most probably proceed to the court for prosecution. Eighty per cent of these offers are accepted, and this has had the result of removing many cases from the district court in particular.

Although these schemes deal with minor offences, they are nevertheless of importance and have made a substantial impact, together with the vehicle defect rectification scheme, on the number of cases proceeded against. They are not the only alternatives to prosecution. Use has been made also of other types of diversion, including that to psychiatric or reparation and mediation schemes, but this has been limited partly because there are very few psychiatric or reparation and mediation schemes in existence. Social work diversion is more widely available, but there is still a limitation on cases that social work departments will accept.

Reparation and mediation schemes have as one of their objectives the greater involvement of the victim in the criminal justice process. In this they pick up on what has been one of the pronounced trends in policy in most Western countries over the last two decades. Recent legislation and policy have responded by trying to create a better balance between, on the one hand, the interests of the offender and, on the other hand, the needs and interests of the victim. The latter have been recognised by a number of developments such as the Criminal Injuries Compensation Scheme, which is run by the government and compensates the victims of certain crimes by the payment of sums of money for the injuries they have suffered.

In terms of penal sanctions, the victim has been recognised by the introduction of compensation orders and, in the context of alternatives to prosecution, this recognition takes the form of reparation and mediation. Reparation and mediation schemes are operated by the procurator fiscal who, in suitable cases, can explore the possibility of offenders not being prosecuted if there is an attempt to 'put right' the damage they have caused to the victim by, for example, apologising, repairing that which was broken, paying a sum of money, or all three. These schemes are voluntary in that neither victim nor offender can be compelled to take part. The mediation aspect refers to the possible involvement of a third party, other than the prosecutor or the victim and offender. The mediator is a volunteer from one of the voluntary agencies that have grown up during the 1980s to represent the interests and rights of the victim and to offer concrete help to those who have been the victims of a crime.

As yet, in Scotland, the mediation and reparation schemes deal with relatively minor crimes and offences, but it is very likely that their scope will be expanded in the future.

The result of these alternatives to prosecution, added to the number of fiscal warnings given (a formal warning in writing by the fiscal), is that the number of persons prosecuted in the courts has actually fallen, although the number of crimes and offences recorded has increased. In 1986, 822,000 crimes and offences were recorded and 501,000 were cleared up; 204,933 persons were proceeded against in court. The corresponding figures for 1994 were 991,000 crimes and offences recorded, 618,000 cleared up but only 178,292 persons proceeded against in court.

The White Paper, *Firm and Fair* (1994), contained a number of proposals to develop further diversions from prosecution and these have been legislated for in the Criminal Justice (Scotland) Act 1995. In particular, Section 66 of the Act will allow diversion schemes provided by local authorities to be included in the scope of the 100 per cent central government funding arrangements for criminal justice social work services (see Chapter 5). The Act also introduces measures to consolidate and expand the use of fixed penalties by the procurators fiscal. It is proposed to increase the level of the fiscal fine from its present ceiling of £25 to four levels: £25, £50, £75 and £100. The requisite level will be determined by fixed points which it is proposed to introduce in the future. It will be possible, as it is now, to pay these fines by instalment.

These examples illustrate the use of prosecutors' discretion on the grounds of public interest. It ought to be said that not all criminal justice systems allow public prosecutors to act in this way. In some systems the prosecutor must, in theory, proceed in every case if there is sufficient evidence. Such systems are said to work on the 'principle of legality'. Systems which allow the prosecutor the sort of discretion discussed are said to work on the 'principle of opportunity or expediency'. A good example of a country which operates on the legality principle is Italy; Scotland and the Netherlands are examples of prosecution systems based on the principle of opportunity.

The result of the developments described above is that in Scotland the fiscal now proceeds to prosecution in 58 per cent of those cases in which he or she receives a report from the police.

The discretion of the fiscal is not restricted to the decision to prosecute but extends also to determining the type of procedure under which a case is taken and also the court in which the case will be heard. In contrast to England and Wales, there is no right in Scotland for the accused to elect for trial by jury. The two types of procedure in Scotland for hearing cases are solemn and summary. These will be described in more detail in the next chapter, but the essential difference between them is the presence of a jury to decide the verdict: in solemn procedure a jury will be present, whereas in summary procedure the case will be heard by a judge alone (sheriff court) or justices (district court).

The procurator fiscal may have to bring a prosecution within certain time limits. In solemn procedure, the accused may not be held in custody for more than 80 days without an indictment being served; also, the accused may not be held in custody for more than 110 days without being brought to trial. If the accused is not brought to trial within 110 days then he or she must be released and no further proceedings may be taken. Summary proceedings for statutory offences usually must start within six months of the date on which the offence was committed. There is no such limit for common law offences. If the accused is in custody, he or she may not be detained for more than 40 days without the trial beginning after the complaint was first heard. If this limit is exceeded, then the accused must be released and the charge dropped. In all cases these limits may be varied by application to the court.

Conclusion

This chapter has described the organisational structure of the police and the public prosecution system, outlined the powers of the police and the public prosecutor, and discussed some of the factors which affect the use of discretion in each. As is clear, both the police and the procurator fiscal occupy key positions in the criminal justice process, and their decisions have an immense effect. The police not only largely control who enters the system but, in doing so, directly influence the very image we have of crime. The role of the fiscal is perhaps less visible but is equally important; the fiscal makes crucial decisions which greatly influence the rest of the criminal process. In particular, the fiscal determines who goes on to the next stage and how they go there. Thus, much as the police affect our view of the nature of crime, the fiscal affects our view of the nature of criminal justice in Scotland.

Chapter 5

◆

SOCIAL WORK AND CRIMINAL JUSTICE

A description of a modern Western criminal justice system which did not consider the role of social workers and, more broadly, social work principles, would be incomplete. In Scotland, social workers play a part in every stage of criminal justice from the apprehension of the offender to his or her disposal by the courts. Social workers can be called upon by the police to help with both juveniles and adults who have been detained or with whom they are in contact. Social workers are regularly required to write reports for the criminal courts before sentence is passed, and, thereafter, they will again be closely involved in the prison system and also in the administration of such non-custodial sanctions as probation, fine supervision, supervised attendance orders and the community service order (see Chapters 6 and 7). Also, social workers are central to the juvenile justice system where they play a key role in the Children's Hearing.

While social workers perform similar tasks elsewhere, the precise nature of those undertaken by social workers in Scotland is governed by a series of distinctive administrative, cultural and legal relationships that have grown up over time. The purpose of this chapter is to describe these relationships and the recent developments in them.

The Wider Background

The wider background to the role of social work in criminal

justice is the emergence, in the nineteenth century, of the idea that criminals should be reformed or treated rather than punished. At first, the ideas that inspired this conception were largely religious in origin. Towards the end of the nineteenth century, however, the emphasis on religious ideas faded, to be replaced by a conception of the criminal and of crime as the products of the causal interaction of damaging personal and social circumstances. The idea of treating or rehabilitating criminals developed from this and came to be understood as the attempt to deal with the criminal by trying to change his or her behaviour by scientific means. The social worker fitted into this as one of the experts who possessed the knowledge and skills to bring about this change.

The Contemporary Context: The Social Work (Scotland) Act 1968 to the Present Day

In Scotland, these developments culminated in the 1960s in the advocacy of a particular philosophy of how criminal justice social work services ought to be provided. This philosophy stressed that offending, whether on the part of adults or juveniles, should be seen in the broad context of the person's social circumstances and that the provision of social work services to the criminal justice system ought to be organised so as to reflect this. In some of the literature this idea has come to be known as the 'Kilbrandon idea', named after the report of a government committee set up to consider how the then criminal justice process dealt with children and young persons, but it is probably more accurately to be known as 'generic social work practice'. Although recent developments have modified this original idea to some extent, it is still the basis of the present scheme and can thus properly be seen as the source of the distinctive arrangements governing the delivery of social work services to criminal justice in Scotland.

Generic Social Work Practice and the 1968 Act

As was said, the essence of the generic idea is that crime and delinquency are best seen and understood in the broader context of the other social and personal problems that accompany them. It was argued that social work intervention was more likely to be effective if it dealt with these broader social and personal problems than if it concentrated on crime and offending behaviour alone.

This philosophy, together with the administrative and legal changes needed to give it effect, was put in place by the Social Work (Scotland) Act 1968, which still remains the fundamental legislation in the area. Perhaps the best-known outcome of this Act is the Children's Hearings which came into operation in 1972 and are described in Chapter 9. The 1968 Act, however, also had significant consequences for the organisation of social work services for adults and young offenders. Perhaps the most important of these was the abolition of a separate probation service in Scotland. Until the 1968 Act came into effect, probation in Scotland was organised in essentially the same manner as in England and Wales. Although the probation service was organised locally, it was separated from other social work services provided by the local authority. The probation officer was regarded as a servant of the court who supplied social work skills designed specifically with offenders in mind. While social workers and probation officers shared certain social work principles, they were trained separately and in some respects had distinctive outlooks on their respective roles.

The effect of the 1968 Act was to bring about a far-reaching change in these arrangements in Scotland. The Act made local authorities responsible for the tasks previously carried out by the probation service; indeed, as was said, the probation service was abolished altogether. The local authorities became responsible not only for the provision of social work services for offenders, but also for their funding (the exception to this was social work services for prisons, which remained fully funded by central government). The generic idea was put into effect in that these services for offenders came to be supplied by the area social work team. One consequence of these new administrative arrangements was that the services for offenders had to compete for priority with all the other types of service the area team was to deliver.

The generic idea had clear advantages and was at the time seen by many as progressive. It placed crime and offending behaviour in a broad social and welfare context, but this, in itself, had the disadvantage of dispersing the more focused attention both the courts and the offender received from the specialised skills and dedicated resources offered by a separate probation service. It has been argued that the long-term impact of the generic idea was to lower the status of probation work with the result that the provision of criminal justice social work services became less effective and undervalued (Moore and Wood 1992).

The National Objectives and Standards for Social Work in the Criminal Justice System

Recent changes in the delivery of criminal justice social work services have tried to address some of the perceived problems of the previous scheme while keeping in place its basic structure. The two most important changes are, first, that since April 1991, central government has provided 100 per cent funding to local authorities for these services. The second important change was the publication in March 1991 of the National Objectives and Standards. National Standards have been in place for community service from 1989, with other services included in 1991. The objective of both is to improve the standard of services for all the groups who use them so as to ensure better value for money. The National Objectives' aim is also to encourage the users of social work services, including the criminal courts, to have greater confidence in the quality and effectiveness of these services. They do this by setting out a clear statement of what services are available, together with a statement of the standards by which the quality of their delivery is to be assessed.

To these ends, the National Objectives and Standards define what the aims of social work in this area should be and describe in detail the type of social work practice necessary to achieve these aims. The document provides a general Statement of Objectives and then proceeds to offer advice and guidance on how these are to be put into effect in the specific areas in which social workers are called upon to deliver services. The Statement is given at paragraph 12 of the document and is:

1. to enable a reduction in the incidence of custody, whether on remand, at sentence, or in default of financial penalty, where it is used for lack of a suitable, available community-based social work disposal;

2. to promote and enhance the range and quality of community-based social work disposals available to the courts and ensure that they are managed and supervised in such a manner that they have the confidence of courts, the police and the public at large;

3. to ensure that social work disposals are provided to the courts or other agencies in such a way that the full range of disposals is available when required so that the most appropriate one can be used;

4. to ensure that a range of disposals is provided in such a way as to provide courts with a range of options, particularly when dealing with the persistent offender;

5. to give priority to the development of community-based social work disposals and other services to young adult offenders;

6. to promote the development of schemes to enable the courts to grant bail in an increased number of cases unless there are overriding grounds against doing so;

7. to provide and facilitate services for prisoners, and their families, to help them prepare for release from custody, and to assist them to resettle in the community on release, within the law;

8. to help offenders tackle their offending behaviour and assist them to live socially responsible lives within the law, whenever appropriate with the involvement and support of their families, friends and other resources in their community;

9. to assist the families of offenders where family life suffers as a consequence of offending behaviour;

10. to promote, provide and facilitate the development of schemes for diverting accused persons from prosecution to social work in those cases where there is sufficient evidence to prosecute but it is not deemed necessary to do so in the public interest;

11. to promote and assist the development of services to the victims of crime;

12. to promote and assist action to reduce and prevent crime.

These are far-reaching objectives which cover the full range of social work services provided. The Statement is of interest because it indicates the matters which were seen to be of concern and which formed the background to the composition of the document. The document was the product of a wide-ranging collaboration between central and local government, the police, judiciary and other interested parties. The directors of social work were involved, as were representatives of the Convention of Scottish Local Authorities (COSLA). In this light, it can be seen as a statement of the broad policy objectives to be pursued, not only in the context of the delivery of social work services, but within the criminal justice process more generally.

The Statement, for example, illustrates the importance attached to several general objectives, not only of social work but also of the criminal justice system more generally. These include a reduction in the use of custody in suitable cases; the emphasis to be laid on community-based sanctions and the importance of the community in crime reduction and prevention and in the reintegration of offenders; the importance of support for prisoners' families; the promotion of alternatives to prosecution; and the enhancement of the position of the victim.

In more specific social work terms, the key provision is perhaps that related to encouraging offenders to address their offending behaviour. This provision reflects a belief, based on research, that offending behaviour can be successfully and effectively tackled by encouraging offenders to accept responsibility for their actions and to take measures to avoid its recurrence by addressing the underlying problems. The role of the social worker is to facilitate both these things by a careful and close supervision that is consistent also with the broader objectives and demands of the criminal justice process. It is the pursuit of these objectives which guides the delivery of social work services at each stage of involvement from the provision of social enquiry reports to the court, to the administration of community-based sanctions like probation and community service, to the delivery of social work services to prisoners released subject to supervision.

It is important to point out, however, that the National Standards do not have the force of law but, through Section 5 of the 1968 Act, adherence can be made a condition of payment of grant. Neither the Statement of Objectives, nor the detailed descriptions provided of how social workers are to discharge their duties in specific areas, have the status of legislation. Rather, the document is a full account of what social workers are encouraged to regard as good practice. The section on probation, for instance, provides an elaborate conception of the different contexts in which probation can work. It distinguishes between probation orders of varying degrees of intensity, from standard probation orders, to those with requirements attached to them, to what is called 'intensive probation' suitable for the more serious offenders. It also describes in some detail what are known as 'action plans'. These are plans which set out, for the benefit of the court, the social worker's conception of how a probation order is to be administered so as to derive maximum value and effect.

Research is currently under way to evaluate the implementation, impact and effectiveness of the 100 per cent funding arrangements and the National Standards. Individual sections of the National Standards are being updated regularly to reflect experience gained and changes in statutory provision. One consequence of their implementation that can already be observed is the general reinvigorating effect that they, along with other developments such as enhanced training for social workers, have had on the delivery of criminal justice social work services.

Chapter 6

◆

THE CRIMINAL COURTS OF SCOTLAND

This chapter will examine the structure of the criminal courts in Scotland and describe how they operate. This description will be set in a broader context by discussing the more general issue of sentencing policy and its relationship to the use of the penal sanctions that the courts have at their disposal. The chapter begins, however, by reiterating the distinction between the main types of procedures used in the criminal courts.

Solemn and Summary Procedure

Solemn procedure is used in the most serious cases tried in the criminal courts. In solemn procedure, trial, in the case of a plea of not guilty, is before a judge and a jury of 15 lay people, and the alleged crime is set out in a document called an indictment. The judge decides questions of law and the jury questions of fact; it is the jury which delivers the verdict in each case, and they may reach their decision by a simple majority of not less than eight. Summary procedure is used in the less serious cases. In summary procedure, the judge sits alone and decides both questions of law and of fact. The offence is set out in a document called a summary complaint. Solemn procedure can be used in both the High Court and the sheriff court. Summary procedure is used in the sheriff court and in the district court. The vast majority of criminal cases in Scotland are heard on summary procedure.

There are three levels of criminal court in Scotland. The

lowest level of court is the district court; in the middle tier is the sheriff court; at the pinnacle of the hierarchy is the High Court of Justiciary.

The District Court

District courts were established by the District Courts (Scotland) Act 1975 and are the administrative responsibility of the local authority. The judges in these courts are called justices and are lay individuals who have been appointed either by the Secretary of State or by the local authority, or who were justices before the new structure began in 1975. The justices sit alone or in threes (known as benches) and are guided in their deliberations in questions of law by the clerk of the court or convenor, both of whom are legally qualified. The local authority may also appoint, subject to the approval of the Secretary of State, a stipendiary magistrate who must be a professional lawyer with at least five years' experience; the stipendiary magistrate has the same summary criminal jurisdiction and powers as has a sheriff. Only Glasgow has stipendiary magistrates sitting in the district court.

District courts can deal only with summary criminal matters, and the justices are able to impose up to 60 days' imprisonment and a fine of up to £2,500, subject to certain additional sentencing powers provided under Section 60 of the Criminal Justice (Scotland) Act 1995.

The Sheriff Court

The sheriff court is the busiest of all the criminal courts and has both extensive criminal and civil jurisdiction. The sheriff is a professional lawyer who has been in practice for at least ten years either as a solicitor or as an advocate. There are six sheriffdoms in Scotland, each of which is subdivided into sheriff court districts, there being 49 in all.

The sheriff has jurisdiction in both summary and solemn criminal cases. While sitting in a summary court, the sheriff may impose prison sentences of up to three months or in some special cases up to twelve months. The sheriff may impose fines of up to £5,000 for a common law offence or up to the maximum allowed in statutory offences. In solemn procedure, the sheriff may impose a prison sentence of up to three years, but the sheriff has power to remit a case to the High Court for sentence if it is thought that a longer sentence is required in a common law crime. In common law crimes, the sheriff may impose an unlimited fine.

The High Court of Justiciary

This is the supreme criminal court in Scotland and sits in Edinburgh and on circuit in other major cities and towns. It consists of the Lord Justice General, Lord Justice Clerk and all the judges of the Court of Session. It only hears cases on indictment and has exclusive jurisdiction in crimes such as murder, rape and treason.

As well as disposing of particular cases, the High Court also plays a more general role in matters of sentencing. Its decisions in criminal cases influence the practice of the lower courts, and the Lord Justice Clerk has, by tradition, been seen to have a particular role in this regard. The High Court can also pass Acts of Adjournal that regulate the operations and procedures of the lower courts. The Court also has declaratory powers. These are powers that enable the Court to 'make new law' by, for example, extending an existing common law crime to cover an area of behaviour where it had not previously been applied; in this way the Court creates 'new' crimes without recourse to legislation. The recent creation of the crime of rape in marriage is an example.

The High Court also sits as a court of appeal in criminal matters. Its powers in this regard are described in the final section of this chapter.

The Volume of Work in the Courts

The greatest numbers of persons were disposed of in 1994 by the sheriff court, at 97,701 cases. The High Court disposed of 1,164 cases, and the district courts of 78,968. One of the more notable trends in the period between 1982 and 1994 was the decrease in the number of persons called to the sheriff court: 141,262 persons in 1982, but by 1994 this had decreased to 97,701. This change probably reflects the decrease in the number of persons being prosecuted in the courts by the procurator fiscal by being dealt with under one of the 'diversion' schemes mentioned in Chapter 5. As a result of the removal of minor cases from the district court and the transfer of cases from the sheriff to the district court, there has been an increasing proportion of more serious sentences in both the district and the sheriff courts.

The Position of the Accused before the Commencement of Court Proceedings

Before examining what happens in the criminal court, it is necessary to describe two important legal provisions that greatly affect the position of an individual who has been charged with a crime but whose case has yet to be heard. These provisions are legal aid and bail.

Legal Aid

Legal aid is the provision made from public funds whereby individuals on low and modest incomes are given access to the legal system. The underlying principle is that justice ought not to be denied to a person because he or she cannot afford the cost.

Legal aid in Scotland is governed by the Legal Aid (Scotland) Act 1986. Legal aid administration is largely the responsibility of the Scottish Legal Aid Board, which is an independent statutory body.

Criminal legal aid is available for prosecutions brought in the district court, the sheriff court, the High Court of Justiciary and in appeals from all criminal courts. There is no absolute entitlement to legal aid. The 1986 Act sets out the statutory tests which must be met before criminal legal aid is granted. The courts decide on whether to grant legal aid in solemn proceedings or in summary proceedings, where a person who has not previously been sentenced to imprisonment or detention has been convicted and the court is considering a sentence of imprisonment or detention. To grant legal aid, the court must be satisfied, after consideration of the person's financial circumstances, that he or she cannot meet the expenses of the case without undue hardship. In all other summary proceedings, the Scottish Legal Aid Board decides whether to grant legal aid. The Board must be satisfied that it is in the interests of justice to do so and on the grounds of the hardship test.

If a person is held in custody and lacks legal representation, legal aid will normally be available in the form of representation by a duty solicitor. At each district and sheriff court, there will be a number of solicitors present to advise those who are held in custody on their first appearance in the court. If the accused pleads guilty at this time, the solicitor may make a plea in mitigation if this is appropriate. If the case is continued for social work reports, the solicitor will appear again before sentence is passed. If, however, the accused pleads not guilty, then any further legal representation will require a separate application for legal aid which must satisfy the tests mentioned above.

The Scottish Legal Aid Board also decides whether to grant legal aid for a criminal appeal. This will be available if a person satisfies the undue hardship test and, in the case of an appeal under Section 228(1) or Section 442(1)(a) of the Criminal Procedure (Scotland) Act 1975, leave to appeal is granted; or, in the case of an appeal under any other provision of the 1975 Act, the Board is satisfied that it is in the interests of justice. Where the Board refuses criminal legal aid on the grounds that it is not satisfied as regards the interests of justice, and the High Court subsequently determines that it *is* in the interests of justice that legal aid should have been made available, the Board will make such legal aid available.

Bail

Many of the cases that appear before the courts cannot be dealt with at the first calling. In these circumstances they are said to be 'continued'. Unless the court deems it necessary to hold the person in custody, he or she may be released on bail before the next appearance. Bail is the measure that regulates this release in order to ensure reappearance.

The legislation controlling bail is the Bail (Scotland) Act 1980. The purpose of this Act was to replace the previous system of bail, which required the lodging of a sum of money with the court. Although the court can still require money to be lodged in certain circumstances, the nature of which is set out in the Act, the accused can now be released from custody if a pledge is made. The release may be granted only if certain conditions are laid down and the accused undertakes to abide by them.

The conditions set out in the Act aim to establish that the accused will appear at the right time at every diet of the court where his or her offence is being considered; that no offence is committed while on bail; that the accused does not interfere with the witness or obstruct the course of justice in any way; and that the accused is available for any enquiries concerning the case and for the making of any reports in relation to the case that the court sees as necessary. The court is empowered to impose any reasonable specific conditions deemed necessary to ensure the realisation of these ends.

Although the courts have the statutory authority to grant or refuse bail in Scotland, decisions under the Bail etc. (Scotland) Act 1980 are also taken daily by police and prosecutors. When they have charged someone with commission of a crime or an offence, the police have the option of releasing the suspects and reporting them to the prosecutor for possible summons to court, releasing them on a signed undertaking that they will appear at court on a specified date, or detaining them in custody while the prosecutor decides whether they should appear in court.

The factors to be considered in dealing with bail applications were set out by Lord Justice Clerk Wheatley in an opinion issued in 1982. The opinion begins by stating a prejudice in favour of bail but then lists exceptions where the court may refuse to grant bail. These include where there is an existing bail order; or where the person is under the supervision of a social worker as part of a probation order or is on community service or awaiting a deferred sentence. The guidance note is not binding but clearly indicates the circumstances in which a fiscal can oppose the granting of bail and where the court should refuse to grant bail.

The breach of the conditions attaching to bail constitutes a criminal offence that may be punished by a fine or a period of imprisonment. The White Paper *Firm and Fair* proposed measures to strengthen the sanctions available to the court to deal with those who commit a further crime or offence while on bail. The Criminal Justice (Scotland) Act 1995 repeals the separate offence of offending while on bail, which was created by the 1980 Act.

Instead, it allows the court to impose an aggravated sentence for an offence or crime committed while on bail. This penalty will be a fine of up to £1,000 or a period of imprisonment of up to six months (60 days if convicted in the district court), and, when this is done, the court will be required to spell this out separately. The Act also restricts the availability of bail by making it unavailable to those who have a prior conviction for culpable homicide, attempted murder, rape or attempted rape if the accused is now charged with one of these crimes. Bail is already unavailable to those who have previous convictions for murder or treason. The prosecution can request the court to review bail conditions or a decision to grant bail in the light of new information. The 1995 Act introduces a provision to require a person on bail to make him or herself available for the purposes of participating in an identification parade or to enable prints, impressions or samples to be taken under the authority of a warrant.

It is possible for both the prosecution and the defence to appeal against the decision of the court regarding bail.

The Criminal Trial

The idea most people have of how a criminal court works is most probably modelled on the mass-media image of the trial involving prosecution and defence battling over a case in front of a jury. This image bears only a fleeting relationship to the everyday realities of how most criminal cases are disposed of. The vast majority of cases are tried on summary procedure where there is no jury. Research has shown that in most cases the accused plead guilty to the crime or offence with which they have been charged, and in these circumstances the only issues are those of pleas in mitigation (excuses or explanations put to the court in the hope of achieving a reduction in sentence) and sentencing. In the

Scottish context the media image of the trial is best represented by solemn procedure, although it must be remembered that only 2 per cent of cases are dealt with in this way and even fewer (1 per cent) involve a trial where evidence is led.

While solemn procedure is rare, it does, however, reflect a basic feature of the Scottish system and, in that sense, has a much wider relevance. The basic feature reflected is the conception of the trial as a contest in which the truth emerges through the 'battle' engaged in by the two sides. This model of criminal justice is described as 'adversarial' and is normally contrasted with the 'inquisitorial' model of criminal justice. In the inquisitorial model, the judge plays a more active role than is the case in the adversarial model. In the former the judge conducts inquiries into the case and plays an active part in examining the witness; in the latter, the judge is more of a neutral umpire who is there to ensure 'fair-play' between the parties.

In historical terms, the adversarial model is seen to be a product of the English system and the inquisitorial model a product of the continental European systems. As was said in Chapter 3, the Scots system exhibits aspects of both. Although its system of trial is essentially adversarial, there are features of its prosecution system that are inquisitorial, such as the absence of the right of the accused to elect for a trial. The same can also be said of some of the earlier stages of solemn procedure, such as first examination and judicial examination.

The Outcome of Proceedings

In this section, the outcome of the criminal proceedings will be examined. First, however, it is necessary to look at the various outcomes possible in a criminal trial.

There are three verdicts possible in Scots criminal law. These are guilty, not guilty and not proven. The last verdict is unique to

Scots criminal law and reflects some of its underlying principles. It is a principle of Scots law that the task of 'proving' whether an accused is guilty of a crime lies with the prosecution. It is the prosecution which must establish its case beyond all reasonable doubt. As lawyers put it, the burden of proof lies with the prosecution. If the prosecution fails to establish its case to this high level, it is possible for this to be reflected in the not proven verdict. The general rule in criminal trials is that the evidence presented has to be corroborated. Corroboration means that each item of evidence presented has to be confirmed by two independent sources. It is thus difficult, but not impossible, for an accused to be convicted on the basis of a confession alone. The not proven verdict has the same practical effect as the not guilty verdict in that the individual is allowed to go free: it thus counts as an acquittal.

In 1994, 11 per cent of those persons called to court were acquitted: 1 per cent were found not proven and 3 per cent not guilty. The remaining acquittals consisted of cases where either a plea of not guilty was accepted or the case was dropped after a person had been called to court. Acquittal rates vary according to the type of crime and offence. Generally, a greater proportion of the more serious crimes charged are likely to result in an acquittal. For example, acquittals are highest of all in crimes such as sexual assault (30 per cent), theft of a motor vehicle (32 per cent), handling offensive weapons (30 per cent) and serious assault (29 per cent). The reason for acquittal does, however, vary. In sexual assaults, 16 per cent were found not guilty and 11 per cent not proven; in handling offensive weapons, 13 per cent were acquitted because the case was either deserted or a plea of not guilty accepted, while 2 per cent were found not proven and 11 per cent not guilty. In theft of a motor vehicle, 24 per cent of persons called to court had a plea of not guilty accepted or a case deserted.

By contrast, acquittals in the least serious offences are much less common; in speeding cases, for instance, only 1 per cent were acquitted and this resulted from pleas of not guilty being accepted or the case being deserted.

Demographic Characteristics of Those against Whom a Charge was Proved

Young persons in the 16–20 age group accounted for 21 per cent of all persons against whom a charge was proved in 1994. This is in disproportion to their distribution in the general population where they account for just 8 per cent of those aged 16 and over. People in the 16–20 age group are much more likely to have more than one charge proved against them in a year than other age groups, and the offences for which they are prosecuted also differ. They are much more likely to be prosecuted for theft by opening lockfast places (58 per cent of persons with a charge proved) and theft of a motor vehicle (66 per cent). Nine per cent of 18- and 19-year-old males in the Scottish population had charges proved against them for a crime, simple assault or breach of the peace on at least one occasion in 1994. The rate for females was much lower at only 1 per cent.

Males are much more likely to have a charge proved against them than females for almost all crimes and offences. Eighty-six per cent of persons against whom a charge was proved in 1994 were male. There are two partial exceptions to this: in the 'other' crimes of violence, which mainly involve neglect of or cruelty to children, women accounted for 46 per cent of all charges proved, and in the 'other' crimes of indecency (mostly prostitution), women accounted for 80 per cent of persons against whom a charge was proved. The only other category in which women figure large (41 per cent) is the 'other' miscellaneous offences which refer mostly to non-payment of TV licences. Males dominated all the other crimes and offences. For example, 100 per cent of those against whom a charge was proved in sexual assaults and 98 per cent in lewd and libidinous practices were male; in drugs-related crimes 91 per cent; simple assault 89 per cent; and breach of the peace 90 per cent.

Sentencing and Penal Sanctions

This section will briefly examine the range of penal sanctions available to a criminal court in Scotland. These sanctions can only be imposed after the accused is found guilty of or pleads guilty to a charge. If a case has been dealt with by solemn procedure, the prosecution must first 'move for sentence' – that is, ask the court to impose a sentence on the guilty offender – before a sentence can be imposed. The main sentences are:

1. **Admonition,** which may be understood as a judicial warning; an admonition counts as a conviction. (In 1994, admonition and caution was the sentence given in 15,967 cases or 10 per cent of the total persons with a charge proved.)

2. **Caution,** which may include lodging a sum of money for a period to guarantee good behaviour. In common law crimes and offences brought on indictment, there is no statutory provision for the maximum amount of money or of the period of time. In statutory offences, taken on solemn procedure, the court has power to order the lodging of a sum of money not exceeding that permitted by the statute and to require good behaviour for up to twelve months. The sheriff court has the same power under summary procedure, and the district court can order the offender to pay a sum of money not exceeding level four on the standard scale (see point 5) and to require good behaviour for up to six months. There is no provision to pay the sum of money found in caution by instalments. If the offender is of good behaviour throughout

the period, the sum of money lodged can be reclaimed together with any interest arising. It should be noted that in summary proceedings, admonition and caution may be made without proceeding to conviction.

3. Probation, which is a non-custodial sentence in which the offender is placed under the supervision and guidance of a social worker. The Criminal Justice (Scotland) Act 1995 contains provisions to make the imposition of a probation order count as a conviction in all cases. Probation orders can be made for periods from six months up to three years. Before placing an offender on a probation order, the court must obtain a social enquiry report which is a report on the offender's personal and social circumstances prepared by a social worker. Legally, reports must be supplied within four weeks; three weeks when remanded; or eight weeks on cause shown. These time limits have been set by the National Standards. The judge must explain the nature of the conditions attaching to a probation order to the offender and obtain his or her agreement to these conditions before imposing the order (1994: 6,011 or 4 per cent of all disposals).

4. Community service order, which has been available since 1979 and consists of a requirement that the offender will undertake unpaid work in the community under the supervision of a social worker. The minimum number of hours is 40 and the maximum 300. Before making an order, the court must be satisfied that four conditions are fulfilled. These are: (1) that the offender consents, (2) that community service is available in the area where the offender resides, (3) that the court is satisfied that the offender is a suitable person for community service, and (4) that suitable work is available (1994: 5,430 or 3 per cent of all disposals). The 1995 Act contains a number of measures to strengthen the conditions under which community-based sanctions are served. These include a provision which will make committing an offence against any person for whom, or premises at which, an offender undertook unpaid work as part of a community service or probation order, an aggravation of that offence. The same provision will apply to any such offence committed within three months of completing a community service order.

5. Fine, which is the most commonly used sanction especially in courts of summary jurisdiction. In determining the amount to be fined, the court is required to take into account the means of the offender. Since 1975, the money amount of fines has been expressed in terms of a standard scale which contains five levels. At present these are:

Level 1 £200
Level 2 £500
Level 3 £1,000
Level 4 £2,500
Level 5 £5,000

These sums may be altered by the Secretary of State in order to accommodate inflation and other changes in the value of money. The amount that can be fined in common law crimes is limited only by the sentencing powers of the court in which the offence is heard.

In most cases, offenders are allowed time to pay fines and may also be allowed to pay their fine by instalments. Those offenders who pay their fines by these methods may be placed on a fines supervision order under the supervision of a social worker. These orders are more common for offenders under 21 years of age. If offenders fail to pay their fine, they may be called to a means-enquiry court which may vary the conditions attaching to the payment of the fine or send the offender to prison for non-payment. The court must obtain a further report from the fine supervision officer before committing the offender to jail if the offender was under a supervision order. A young offender cannot be detained for non-payment until a report from the social worker has been obtained and considered by the court. Before imposing imprisonment for non-payment, the court may order a report from a fine supervision officer. If an offender is imprisoned for non-payment, the period spent in prison is determined by the amount of fine outstanding according to a scale contained in the Criminal Procedure (Scotland) Act 1995. The period is reduced by any amount that may have been paid before the court imposed imprisonment for default. The mean fine imposed in 1994 was £138, half of all fines imposed were £100 or less, and a quarter were £50 or less (1994: 112,428 or 71 per cent of all disposals).

6. Supervised attendance order, which is a new measure introduced by the Law Reform (Miscellaneous Provisions) (Scotland) Act 1990 in connection with fine enforcement. The aim of this order is to provide the court with a mechanism of dealing with fine-defaulters by a means other than imprisonment if this is seen as appropriate. These orders require the offender to attend a place of supervision for between 10 and 60 hours and to undertake activities as directed by the supervising officer. The Criminal Justice (Scotland) Act 1995 extends the upper limit to 100 hours and introduces the use of supervised attendance orders as a first instance disposal for 16- and 17-year-olds in place of a fine, where the court considers the offender would be unable to pay.

7. Compensation order on the offender and in favour of the victim. The compensation order was introduced by the Criminal Justice (Scotland) Act 1980. It must be given priority over the fine if both are competent but the offender does not have the means to meet both. The monies paid in compensation go to the victim of the crime or offence. The amount to be paid in compensation is determined by a number of factors: the court is required to take into account the offender's means, the damage caused by the offence, and the conduct of the victim. As a result of a case taken on solemn procedure, the sum is unlimited. In the case of summary procedure, the upper limit is determined by the powers the court possesses to fine in common law crimes (1994: 1,659 or 1 per cent where the order was the main penalty, but more than 329 or 5 per cent where the order was awarded as the main or secondary penalty).

8. Imprisonment of the offender but only if he or she is over 21. Offenders under 21 can receive custodial sentences as a period of detention in a young offenders institution. The use of imprisonment for offenders who have not previously received such a sentence is restricted by the court having to be sure that no other alternative is suitable. The determination of this will typically involve the consideration of a social enquiry report but is, of course, greatly influenced by the gravity of the crime or offence for which the offender has been found guilty. The length of the sentence will be determined by a number of considerations, including the seriousness of the offence, previous criminal record and any relevant statutory provisions.

9. Young offenders institutions (YOIs), which are penal establishments for young offenders. If the offender is between 16 and 21, it is possible for him or her to be sentenced to a young offenders institution. The sentence can be no longer than that which would have been awarded if the offender was an adult (in 1994, 4,426 or 3 per cent of all disposals of young offenders resulted in a custodial sentence). The same year, half of all custodial sentences to both imprisonment and a young offenders institution were for three months or less. The mean length of determinate custodial sentence was 214 days. This figure is greater than the former figure just quoted because of the effect of the small number of long sentences imposed. It should be noted that murder attracts a mandatory life sentence which is wholly indeterminate. (In 1994, imprisonment constituted 11,500 or 7 per cent of all disposals, and detention in a young offenders institution 3 per cent.)

10. Absolute discharge/deferred sentence, which it is possible for a court to order. There is no suspended sentence available in Scots criminal law (1994: 430 or 0.3 per cent of persons with a charge proved were absolutely discharged).

Mentally Disordered People

Criminal courts are often called upon to deal with people who are mentally disturbed. There are various paths to be followed. Generally speaking, the prosecution must make the court aware, at the first appearance, of any evidence that an accused is suffering from a mental disorder, and the court can order such an individual to be remanded in a hospital for the purpose of reports. A person can be regarded as being unable to plead or give instructions for his or her defence as a result of mental disorder. If the prosecution accepts this, the case cannot proceed to trial and the person can be detained in a hospital. If this is not accepted by the prosecution, then a plea in bar of trial, on the grounds of insanity, must be considered by the court. If this plea is accepted by the court, the person will be detained in a hospital, including the state mental hospital.

Insanity can also be put forward as a special defence on the grounds that a person must be acquitted if he or she was insane at the time of committing an act that would otherwise be considered a crime. If this defence is successful and the person is acquitted, then he or she is dealt with in the same way as if a plea in bar of trial was accepted; that is, the person is ordered to be detained in hospital. If a mentally disordered person pleads guilty or is found guilty of an offence, then he or she will be dealt with by one of the means described below.

The sentences which can be used to cope with mentally disordered people are hospital and guardianship orders and probation with a condition of treatment. The hospital order is a means of detaining a person in a hospital compulsorily; the guardianship order is used when the court places an individual under the control of a guardian, but not in hospital. In 1994, there were 118 insanity, guardianship or hospital orders made. For crimes, there were 60 orders made in total, most commonly in crimes of violence and in fire-raising and vandalism: 2 were made for homicide, and 14 orders were made as a result of vandalism. Among the offences there were 58 orders in total: 38 orders were made as the result of breach of the peace, and 17 as the result of simple assault.

The government has recently undertaken a comprehensive review of the procedures for dealing with the mentally disordered with the aim of proposing more flexible arrangements. The Criminal Justice (Scotland) Act 1995 introduces these new arrangements, the most important of which are a change in procedure to allow the judicial examination of facts relating to the case and the introduction of a community-based disposal as an alternative to the hospital order which was compulsory for those cases taken on solemn procedure.

Sentencing in Policy and in Practice

The actual sentence handed down in a particular case will depend upon a variety of factors and how they interact. Each sentence will reflect features peculiar to the case, such as the age of the offender, prior criminal record and any special mitigating factors which may be seen to lessen the offender's culpability. Some research suggests that gender also affects the sentence (all these are called offender-related criteria). Above all, however, the sentence will be set to reflect the seriousness of the crime or offence committed – offence-related criteria, as they are known. In the statutory crimes and offences, the statute itself may impose an upper limit, but in the common law crimes there is, of course, no such guidance. In these circumstances, the sentence is limited, in theory, only by the sentencing powers of the court in which the case is heard.

This raises the question of how judges come to evaluate the seriousness of one common law crime against another. The answer is that judges rely upon a sense of seriousness that has been built up over time and which has come to be reflected in what is known as the tariff or the 'going rate'. Judges learn of the tariff or the going rate by experience, through the publication of reported cases and, more recently, also through sentencing seminars. In addition, guidance may come from the High Court, especially sitting as the Court of Appeal.

There is a notable difference between the Scottish and the English Courts of Appeal in this connection. In England, the Court has formulated explicit sentencing guidelines which it expects the lower courts to follow. The Court of Appeal in Scotland has yet to do the same and appears to prefer to influence sentencing practice by the way it deals with particular cases that come before it and by the other means noted above.

The Criminal Justice (Scotland) Act 1995 contains measures to strengthen the role of the Court of Appeal in this regard by introducing a specific statutory power to allow the High Court to issue judgments containing general sentencing guidelines.

Appeals and Miscarriage of Justice

The High Court also sits as the Scottish Court of Criminal Appeal, when there will be at least three judges. As the Court of Appeal, it sits only in Edinburgh. The High Court as the Court of Appeal hears appeals from the district court, the sheriff court and the High Court. The Court will hear appeals against conviction, against sentence or against both on the grounds that there has been a miscarriage of justice.

The Procedure in Appeals

The procedure adopted varies with the nature of the appeal and the procedure under which the case was originally taken. If the appeal arises out of a case that has been dealt with by solemn procedure and is against conviction, the process is begun by lodging a notice of intention to appeal with the Clerk of Justiciary. The final note of appeal is sent to the trial judge, who must respond to the Clerk with a report on the grounds of the appeal as they are stated. Thereafter, the case will be heard by the High Court. The procedure for appeals against sentence is similar except that there is no requirement for a notice of intention to appeal to be lodged.

The method of appeal in cases taken under summary procedure is by stated case. The appellant must apply for a stated case by lodging an application with the clerk of the summary court within one week of the final determination of the proceedings in that court. The application must contain a full statement of all the matter which the appellant wishes to bring under review, including whether there is an appeal against sentence. It is the task of the sheriff – or in the district court, the clerk – to prepare the stated case which, after a period for adjustments, is sent to the High Court. The appellant and his or her solicitor are sent copies of the stated case.

Appeals may also be made by two other means. These are appeals by Bill of Suspension, which is only competent in summary procedure and not solemn procedure, and by Bill of Advocation. It is possible to appeal by Bill of Suspension against conviction and sentence where it is claimed that there has been a miscarriage of justice in the proceedings. In the case of an appeal against sentence, the miscarriage must be of an alleged fundamental nature relating to the imposition of the sentence. In the case of conviction, this method can be used when an appeal, by stated case, would be incompetent or inappropriate. Appeal by Bill of Advocation is open only to the prosecutor if the case was taken on solemn procedure. The appeal can only refer to an alleged irregularity in the court of first instance and cannot be used to review a verdict of acquittal by a jury. In summary procedure, the Bill of Advocation is open to both the prosecutor and the defence.

The High Court also hears bail appeals which arise when there is a dispute concerning the detention of a person held in custody prior to trial. These disputes can be over the conditions imposed if bail is granted. The prosecution as well as the defence can appeal against bail decisions. In bail cases, there will be only one judge sitting who will hear the case in Chambers.

The Criminal Justice (Scotland) Act 1995 introduced a single sift judge system in which a single judge is able to examine appeals to see if they have merit, which includes a judgment on the adequacy of the drafting of the grounds of appeal. If the applicant is refused leave to appeal by the single judge, it will be possible for the application to be renewed for hearing before the full Court. These measures are backed up by new statutory changes which require an appellant to obtain leave to appeal, for appeals arising from both solemn and summary procedure. The number of judges needed to form a quorum for the hearing of appeals has also been reduced by the 1995 Act. At present, three judges are required to form a quorum, but it is proposed to reduce this to two in cases where the appeal is against sentence. Appeals against conviction will continue to be heard by at least three judges. These measures will be put into effect by the Criminal Justice (Scotland) Act 1995.

The Powers of the High Court in Cases of Appeal

The powers of the High Court in cases of appeal vary with the nature of the appeal and the procedure under which it has been brought. The Court may dispose of an appeal brought against conviction on solemn procedure in three ways. It may affirm the decision of the trial court; it may set the verdict aside and either quash the conviction or substitute an amended verdict of guilty; or it may set aside the verdict and grant authority for a new prosecution to be brought. In the case of appeals against sentence, the Court may affirm the sentence or it may quash the sentence and pass another one which can be more or less severe.

The Court can deal with appeals by stated case in four ways. The case can be remitted to the trial court with its opinion and a direction as to what the Court should do; the Court can affirm the verdict of the trial court; it may set aside the verdict and either quash the conviction or substitute an amended verdict of guilty; or it can set aside the verdict and grant an authority to bring a new prosecution.

The powers of the prosecution to appeal against the decision of a court are more limited. In addition to those mentioned above, the prosecutor, in summary cases, has a right to appeal against an acquittal or against a sentence but only on a point of law.

There is no appeal in criminal cases to the House of Lords.

Other Means of Dealing with Miscarriage of Justice

There are three other means by which a miscarriage of justice may be handled:

1. The Secretary of State has a right to refer cases to the High Court for consideration, where they will be dealt with as appeals. This is a rare occurrence and is normally used when new evidence arises after an earlier appeal has failed.

2. While there is no right of appeal available to the Crown against the verdict of a jury, it is possible for the Lord Advocate, when there has been an acquittal, to refer a case to the High Court for consideration on a point of law relating to the charge. The Criminal Justice (Scotland) Act 1995 has brought about a change in that the Lord Advocate can refer a case on a point of law to the High Court regardless of the outcome of the trial.

3. Finally, it is possible to appeal to the nobile officium of the High Court. This is a power the High Court possesses to hear appeals that arise out of extraordinary or unforeseen circumstances, and is used to prevent injustice or oppression. The method is by petition and the appeal is heard by a bench of at least three judges.

Chapter 7

_____◆_____

THE USE OF PENAL SANCTIONS IN SCOTLAND

This chapter will examine the actual use made of the sentences available to the criminal courts. The objectives are to provide a description of how often the different types of sentence are used, to look at what types of crimes are punished by what type of penal sanction, and to note any changes. All figures are taken, unless otherwise indicated, from the relevant volumes of the official statistics (in the main, *Criminal Proceedings in the Scottish Courts, 1994*).

1950–94

Figures 7.1, 7.2 and 7.3 record changes in the use of the main penal sanctions for the period 1950–94 in terms of the total number of charges proved. Figure 7.1 records the use of all custodial measures and the fine, Figure 7.2 records separately the use of custody, and Figure 7.3 records the use of admonition and caution, probation, community service orders and compensation orders.

In terms of their frequency of use, a comparison of Figures 7.1, 7.2 and 7.3 shows that the fine dominates all other sanctions. It is followed, for most of the period, by admonition and caution, then by custodial measures, then by probation, community service orders and finally by compensation orders. The predominance of the fine is attributable in part to the frequency of its use in the offence (rather than crime) groups, where it is normally used in over 80 per cent of all cases, but reflects also its common usage in the various groups of crimes where, in 1994, it accounted for 48 per cent of all penalties.

As Figure 7.1 illustrates, the shape of the curve for the fine closely follows that for charges proved, which suggests that any change in the former is largely a reflection of changes in the latter. The notable dip in both from the early 1980s is the result of the introduction of the various alternatives to prosecution for motor vehicle offences – a category in which the fine has always dominated. The use of custodial measures, as represented in Figure 7.1, has remained relatively constant throughout this period, with there being a slight increase overall. While Figure 7.1 gives an accurate view of the use of custody in relation to the the total number of charges proved and the use made of the fine,

Figure 7.1 The use of custodial measures and the fine, 1950–94.

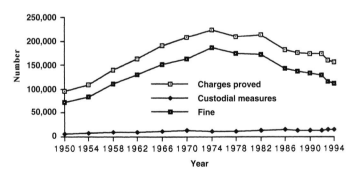

Source: Criminal Proceedings in Scottish Courts.

it tends to hide the significant increase in the absolute number of custodial sentences. Figure 7.2, below, records this increase.

As can be seen from Figure 7.2, the use made of custody has risen significantly in absolute terms. There have been three periods within which its use has increased: the period from 1950 to 1970, then from 1978 to 1986 and, more recently, from 1990 onwards. It is to be noted, however, that its use declined from 1970 to 1978 and from 1986 to 1990; there was also a levelling-off in its use from the late 1950s to the early 1960s.

It can be seen from Figure 7.3 that the use of caution and admonitions has undergone a change in the period. Their use increased significantly in the 1950s and 1960s, reaching a plateau in the early 1970s with a high point in 1982, since when their use has declined, most noticeably from the mid-1980s. The position with regard to the use of probation is a little different. It should be observed that probation appears, from the graph, never

Figure 7.2   The use of custody, 1950–94.

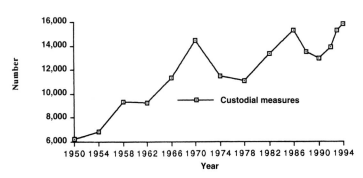

Source: Criminal Proceedings in Scottish Courts.

to have been a popular sanction with the criminal courts and seems to have become increasingly unpopular as time went on. As can be seen, the use of probation decreased considerably after 1970, and it was not until the late 1980s that there were any clear signs of an upward trend. By 1994 the use of probation had risen to 4 per cent of cases in which a charge had been proved. It should be noted that the option of including community service work as a condition of a probation order is now available to all sheriff courts.

The fall in the use of probation seems most clearly to be related to the abolition of the separate probation service by the Social Work (Scotland) Act of 1968. To judge from the trends described here, the courts appear to have lost some faith in probation as a penal measure in response to the provisions of that Act. It must also be remembered, however, that the Act introduced the Children's Hearings system, which had the

Figure 7.3 The use of admonition and caution, probation, community service and compensation orders, 1950–94.

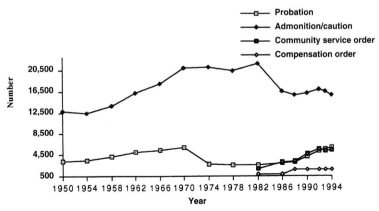

Source: Criminal Proceedings in Scottish Courts.

105

consequence of removing most juvenile offenders from the criminal courts; as probation was used to deal with juveniles, this would have markedly reduced its use. The introduction of the National Objectives and Standards for social work in the criminal justice system in 1991 may help to increase the use of probation by the courts, but it is still too early to make a judgment.

As Figure 7.3 shows, the use of the community service order has increased significantly since its introduction, and it is now used to deal with 3 per cent of cases in which a charge has been proved. The increase in the use of the compensation order as the main penalty has not been so marked. As Figure 7.3 shows, the compensation order appears not to have been used much in the first years until the late 1980s when, in relative terms, its use increased significantly, since when it has remained constant. As a main penalty, the compensation order is used in 1 per cent of cases in which a charge is proved. The compensation order is, however, used as a secondary penalty also. In this context, 4 per cent of cases in 1994 were dealt with by a compensation order.

While this analysis gives a general picture of what has happened during the period, it is not sufficiently detailed to show if there have been any changes in the use made of penalties with respect to particular crimes and offences. In order to construct a more detailed picture, a number of particular crimes, from the main groups, have been selected for closer examination.

Figure 7.4 comprises six bar charts which illustrate the use of penalties in five crimes and one offence. Two of the crimes – serious assault and robbery – are classed as crimes of violence; fraud and housebreaking are classified as crimes of dishonesty; sexual assault (consisting of a number of crimes – rape, intent to rape and indecent assault) is classed as a crime of indecency; and breach of the peace as a miscellaneous offence (simple assault has been added to breach of the peace).

Figure 7.4   The use of penal sanctions in five selected crimes and one offence.

(a)   Serious assault: use of sanctions, 1950–94.

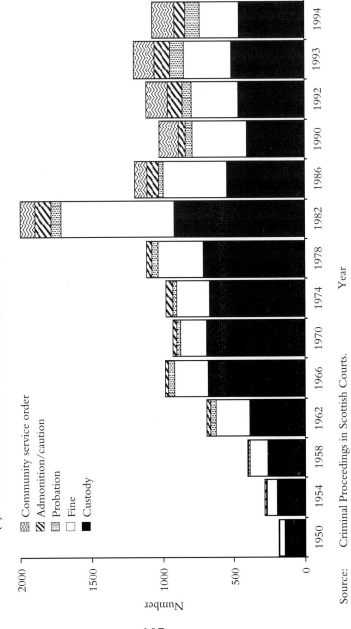

Source: Criminal Proceedings in Scottish Courts.

(b) Robbery: use of sanctions, 1950–94.

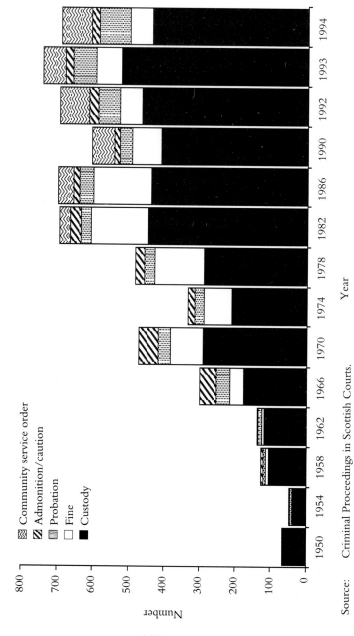

Source: Criminal Proceedings in Scottish Courts.

107a

(c) Sexual assault: use of sanctions, 1950–94.

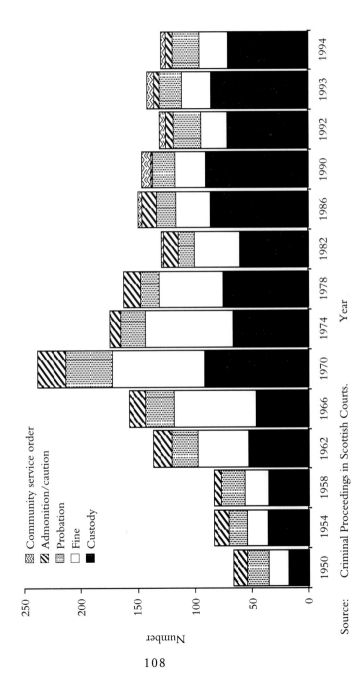

Source: Criminal Proceedings in Scottish Courts.

(d) Housebreaking: use of sanctions, 1950–94.

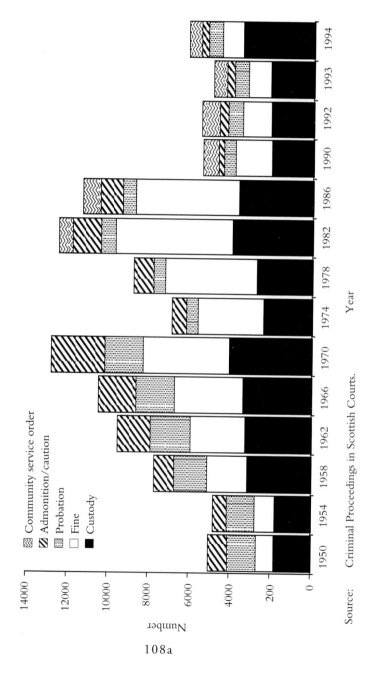

Source: Criminal Proceedings in Scottish Courts.

108a

(e) **Fraud: use of sanctions, 1950–94.**

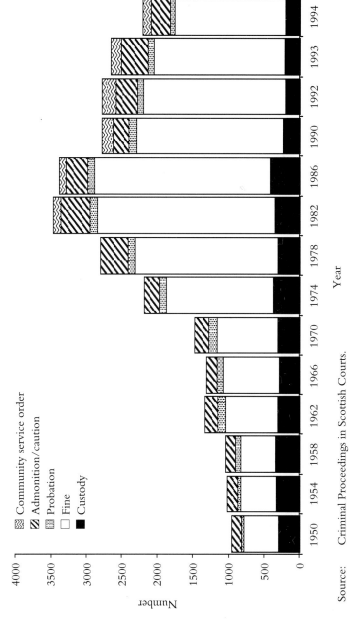

Source: Criminal Proceedings in Scottish Courts.

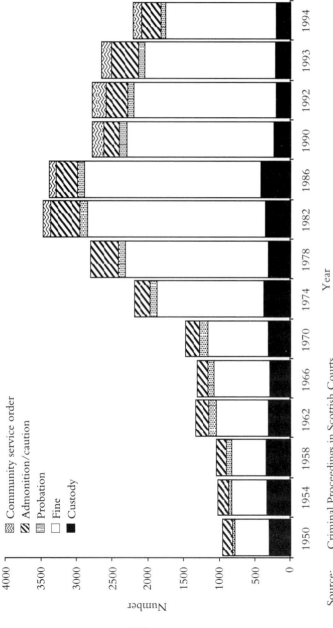

(f) **Breach of the peace/simple assault: use of sanctions, 1950–94.**

Legend:
- ▨ Community service order
- ▨ Admonition/caution
- ▦ Probation
- ☐ Fine
- ■ Custody

Year

Number

Source: Criminal Proceedings in Scottish Courts.

109a

Comparison of the bar charts in Figure 7.4 shows the differences in sentencing practice that exists between different crimes. For example, fraud and housebreaking have noticeably different sentencing patterns, although both are classed as crimes of dishonesty. Whereas fraud has been dealt with mainly by the fine, in housebreaking, no one penalty dominates over the period. The bar chart for fraud shows that the use of the fine has increased over the period and the use of custody has fallen off. The chart for housebreaking records an increasing reliance on the fine over the period but demonstrates also that the pattern of growth is uneven, with the fine being used more in the 1970s, up until the late 1980s, than in 1994. The use of custody, in comparison, remains about the same throughout the period. The penalties which have decreased in use are admonition and caution. As can be seen, the use of community service orders has grown substantially in the 1980s to deal with housebreaking; it was used to dispose of 13 per cent of such cases in 1994. The same pattern appears in fraud, where there has been a move away from the use of custody to the use of community service orders. There is an interesting contrast in the use of probation to deal with these two crimes of dishonesty. Whereas probation is used to dispose of housebreaking cases throughout the period, this is not so with fraud. It is clear, however, that the courts used probation more to deal with housebreaking up until 1970; after this, the use of probation falls off significantly with there being a slight increase in the 1980s.

The bar charts for the two crimes from the violence group show some similarities to each other. In particular, they show that the use of custody has declined since 1950, especially in serious assault, where its use has diminished by almost 50 per cent. Some of this fall has been taken up by the fine, the usage of which has expanded to 28 per cent; there has also been an increase in the use of probation and admonition. It is to be noted, however, that the use of the fine has declined relative to its use in the early and mid-1980s; community service orders are being increasingly relied upon to deal with serious assault. In 1994, the community service order was used in 14 per cent of such cases. The use of the fine has expanded in robbery cases by a considerable proportion, from being a negligible sanction in 1950 to accounting for 9 per cent of the penalties used for this crime in 1994. This, however, marks a fall from its usage in the period from 1978 to the late 1980s. It is noticeable that the use of community service orders has expanded to deal with robbery. Community service orders are now used in 12 per cent of such cases.

The pattern of sanction usage in sexual assault is distinctive, in that, as the bar chart illustrates, the use of custody has increased over the period from about 24 per cent in 1950 to 54 per cent in 1994. This has caused a decrease in the reliance on the other penalties. This is particularly true of admonition and caution which have dropped from 18 per cent to 4 per cent. Recently, the use of the fine has fallen as well, after an expansion in its use in the 1960s and the 1970s. It is to be noted that probation has been used fairly frequently to deal with this crime throughout the period, and its use now appears to be on the increase after a fall in the period from 1974 to 1982.

The final bar chart illustrates the use of penalties for two offences, breach of the peace (which is in fact a common law crime) and simple assault. As can be seen, there is little change to record over the period. The fine is by far the most used penalty throughout. It can be seen that the use of community service orders is on the increase but to a very limited extent.

The Use of Penalties, 1994

This section will consider in more detail the use of penalties in

1994. Figures 7.5 and 7.6 illustrate the proportionate use of penalties for all crimes and offences, and their proportionate use for each group of crime and offence. Figure 7.5 largely serves to confirm the analysis presented in the first section. It shows the preponderant use of the fine and the position with regard to the other sanctions.

Figure 7.6 shows the proportionate use of the various penalties in relation to the main groups of crimes and offences. The chart makes clear that the proportionate use of custody exceeds the use of the fine in only one group of crimes, that of violence. In all the other crime and offence groups, it is the fine which predominates proportionately. It is perhaps surprising that this pattern holds true even if one compares crimes of indecency with those of dishonesty. As can be seen, the fine is used more in crimes of indecency than in crimes of dishonesty. This is because the crime of indecency most frequently dealt with by the courts is prostitution, a crime which is typically dealt with by the fine. In contrast, the use of custody is proportionately greater in crimes of dishonesty than in those of indecency.

The proportionate use of community service orders varies with the classes of crime. It is used most in crimes of violence and least in crimes of indecency. This contrasts with the use made of probation, which is greatest in crimes of indecency; its use is the same in violence and dishonesty, and the least in vandalism. It is interesting to note that the use of admonition and caution is fairly constant across all the crimes and offences, with the exception of motor vehicle offences.

While Figure 7.6 gives a clear general picture of how the various sanctions are used, it tends to hide the pattern of the proportionate use of sanctions in specific crimes and offences. It is particularly important to look in some detail at the use of sanctions with regard to the crimes because it is here that one

Figure 7.5 The proportionate use of penal sanctions, 1994.

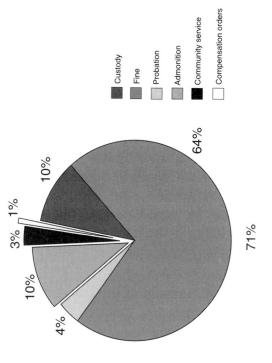

Custody
Fine
Probation
Admonition
Community service
Compensation orders

64%
71%
10%
1%
3%
10%
4%

Source: Criminal Proceedings in Scottish Courts.

Figure 7.6 **The proportionate use of penal sanctions in the groups of crimes and offences, 1994.**

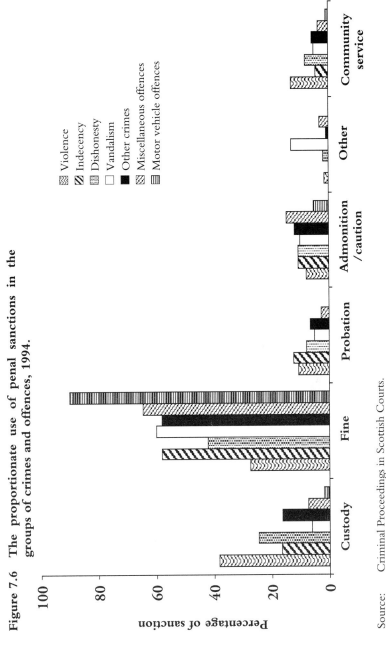

Source: Criminal Proceedings in Scottish Courts.

113a

finds the greatest variation. As was seen earlier, it is also in the crimes that changes over time in the balance between sanctions occur.

Custody is, proportionately, the most common sanction for homicide (82 per cent), robbery (62 per cent), sexual assault (54 per cent), other crimes in the 'other crimes' group (21 per cent), serious assault (41 per cent), housebreaking (44 per cent), fire-raising (28 per cent), lewd and libidinous practices (37 per cent), theft of a motor vehicle (30 per cent) and theft by opening a lockfast place (29 per cent). In terms of the crimes, custody is used least in other crimes of indecency (3 per cent), vandalism (6 per cent), fraud (8 per cent) and drugs (10 per cent).

The fine is used least in two crimes: homicide (4 per cent) and robbery (9 per cent). The crimes for which the fine is used most are other crimes of indecency (75 per cent – mostly prostitution), drugs (75 per cent), fraud (68 per cent), vandalism (64 per cent), shoplifting (52 per cent), other theft (51 per cent) and other crimes of dishonesty (52 per cent).

Community service orders are used most in fire-raising (16 per cent), serious assault and handling offensive weapons (both 14 per cent) and housebreaking (13 per cent). They are used least in shoplifting (3 per cent) and other crimes of indecency (1 per cent). Probation is used most in lewd and libidinous practices (27 per cent), other crimes of violence (31 per cent), fire-raising (25 per cent) and sexual assault (18 per cent). It is used least in drugs (2 per cent) and homicide and fraud (4 per cent). Caution and admonition are used most in other crimes of violence (32 per cent) and crimes against public justice (18 per cent), and least in homicide (2 per cent) and robbery (3 per cent). In 1994 there were 1,659 compensation orders made; most (1,185) were for crimes, and the crime in which they were most commonly used was vandalism (540).

Conclusion

This chapter has looked at the use made of the sentences which are at the disposal of the criminal courts in Scotland. It is clear that the use of particular penalties is influenced by a number of different factors, but the most important seems to be the view taken of the seriousness of the crime or offence by the court. The analysis has also shown the central place occupied by the fine in the criminal justice process; it is the most commonly used sanction for all of the offences and is used to a considerable extent as a sanction for many of the crimes (1994: fire-raising and vandalism (62 per cent), other crimes (59 per cent), crimes of indecency (57 per cent) and dishonesty (44 per cent).

Chapter 8

The Prison System

The purpose of this chapter is to provide an overview of the prison system in Scotland by describing how it is organised, and also by examining the nature of the population incarcerated. The prison system in Scotland presents the observer with a number of apparent contrasts. On the one hand, as will be shown, Scotland imprisons proportionately more of its population than most other countries in Europe; on the other hand, it has introduced some of the most progressive prison regimes to be found anywhere. Scotland thus has a reputation at one and the same time for penal harshness and for penal innovation.

The Organisation of Scotland's Prisons

The Scottish Prison Service (SPS), the headquarters of which is in Edinburgh, is responsible for running Scottish prisons on behalf of the Secretary of State for Scotland who, in turn, is responsible to parliament. The SPS is now an executive agency and is headed by a chief executive, a civil servant, who is responsible to the Secretary of State.

There are 22 penal establishments in Scotland, ranging in size from Barlinnie in Glasgow with over 900 places to Friarton in Perth with about 60. There are also two units for prisoners who present particular management problems, and a National Induction Unit for prisoners beginning sentences of ten years or more. Most establishments accommodate adult male prisoners.

Two are solely for young offenders, while three others have young offenders institutions within the prisons. One establishment, Longriggend, is principally for remand prisoners. Cornton Vale in Stirling is the main establishment solely for women prisoners, although women prisoners can now be housed in two other establishments as well. Establishments are geographically dispersed throughout Scotland, located in both urban and rural areas. The overall design capacity is for around 5,650 prisoners, of which some 200 places are for women, around 1,000 for male young offenders, and the rest for adult males.

It costs £166 million a year to run the SPS and to meet its capital spending programme. The average cost per prisoner place available for use (1995) is approximately £26,700. The SPS has a staff of 4,500 of whom about 200 are based at the headquarters in Edinburgh.

Prisons generally have the dual functions of holding adults on remand and after they have been sentenced. The allocation of a convicted prisoner to a particular prison is dependent upon three principal factors: the prisoner's sentence length, his or hers security category and the type of regime required to help him address his or hers offending behaviour. Short-term prisoners (those serving less than four years) will normally complete their sentence in their local allocation prison; long-term prisoners, as part of the sentence-planning programme, will be given a choice of the closed long-term prisons in which they wish to serve their sentence. In addition to local allocation prisons and closed long-term establishments, there are four open establishments: three for adults and one for young offenders.

Each prison is under the control of a governor who is responsible for the daily running of the establishment. In addition, there will be a number of other senior managers in each prison and a larger number of uniformed staff; there are also

CRIME AND CRIMINAL JUSTICE IN SCOTLAND

social workers, who work in the prison but are not employed by the prison service, and doctors, many of whom are GPs engaged on a part-time basis. The Scottish Prison Service also makes use of psychologists and psychiatrists. Each prison has a chaplain and other visiting clergy, who look after the spiritual welfare of the prisoners. This role is interpreted widely and involves much that could easily be classed as social work. Although attendance at religious services was once compulsory, this is no longer the case.

All convicted prisoners are required to work and have the opportunity to earn modest wages. Prisons aim to provide a range of work opportunities in prison industries (for example textiles, wood-based industries and engineering-based industries) and in work related to running the establishment (catering, laundry and so on). Educational classes are also provided, including remedial education, Standard Grades and Highers and help with Open University degrees. There are now full-time educational officers in two-thirds of all prisons who are assisted by part-time staff. Particular efforts have been made to deal with basic illiteracy, but with varying degrees of success. Vocational training is available at thirteen of the prisons with the aim of providing prisoners with practical skills which may help in the labour market after release: bricklaying, carpentry, hairdressing and upholstery for example. A number of inmates have successfully completed SCOTVEC modules and City and Guilds examinations.

One aspect of prison life to which many inmates attach some importance is the provision of facilities for sport and physical training. Prisons are equipped with gymnasiums and weight-training equipment.

Prison Regimes and the Purposes of Imprisonment

The description of facilities within prisons brings into focus the topic of regimes: how the prison is organised so as to achieve its objectives. The nature of the regime has a direct bearing on the quality of life inside the prison and is closely related to the broader purpose that prisons are seen to serve in society. It is also an area that has been much discussed and debated both within government and by the reform groups which exist to exert pressure on government to improve and change prisons.

A number of factors help explain why there has been this debate about the regime and why it has undergone change. There are two background factors which have exerted particular influence: the first is the decline in the belief that prisons – or, indeed, any penal measure – can rehabilitate offenders, and the second is a concern with the costs of imprisonment, which has surfaced most visibly around attempts to reduce the size of the prison population.

The debate about whether penal measures can rehabilitate offenders has been a recurrent theme of penal policy in most Western countries throughout the twentieth century. The idea of rehabilitation is that it is possible to change offenders' behaviour away from crime by treatment or training. It differs from the concept of punishment because, while rehabilitation sets out to alter behaviour, this is not necessarily true of attempts to punish individuals. Rather, in its pure form, punishment involves inflicting some disadvantage on the criminal to counterbalance that which the criminal has caused to the victim and society generally by committing the crime. If this has the added bonus of stopping the criminal offending again, then this is to be welcomed, but this does not need to be the primary purpose of the punishment for it to be justified.

Penal policy has oscillated between the ideas of punishment and treatment, sometimes laying the greater emphasis on the one and at other times on the other. During the period from 1950 to 1970 (approximately), the idea of treatment was in the ascendant in the UK. It affected the nature of prison regimes in that prisons were seen as places of rehabilitation or, as it was expressed in the prison rules, that the purpose of imprisonment was to help the offender 'to lead a good and useful life'. Since the 1970s, however, rehabilitation has become less popular and the emphasis has been placed more on the prison as a place of punishment. This shift in penal policy, and the attendant change in the nature of the prison regime, was attributable to the interaction of a number of factors. In part, the change was a response to a growing body of research evidence which cast doubt on the ability of rehabilitation to achieve the objective of turning people away from crime; in part, it was related to a yet deeper criticism of the underlying theory of justice upon which rehabilitation was seen to rest.

The most important consequence of this decline in the belief in rehabilitation was the growth, in the late 1960s and the 1970s, of a pervasive scepticism about the penal system in general and the prison in particular. One of the more attractive features of rehabilitation is that it is an essentially optimistic philosophy which seems to say that all individuals, no matter how bad or troublesome, can be made better. The criticisms of it, although well founded in research terms, had the effect of destroying this optimism and of giving rise to a sense of futility about the purposes of the penal system that is best summed up as, in the phrase adopted at the time, 'nothing works'.

The growth of this view coincided with the emergence of the second of the factors mentioned above – the concern about the costs of imprisonment made visible in the worry about the size of the prison population. There has been a consistent rise in the size of the prison population in most Western penal systems. One serious consequence of this has been the growth of overcrowding in prisons. Both Scotland and England and Wales experienced overcrowding, although the problem has been worst in England and Wales.

The joint effect of the interaction of these factors was that, by the late 1970s and during the 1980s, there was a common view that the prison system was in crisis. On the one hand, the prison seemed to lack any justification other than being a place of punishment. Although, of course, this is a perfectly valid view to hold, it does seem negative in that there is a reasonable public expectation that prisons ought to do more, especially to try and reduce crime. On the other hand, overcrowding in prisons made them extremely difficult to manage. The clearest signs of the crisis were the outbreak in the 1980s of disturbances and riots, including hostage-taking, in many prisons in both Scotland and England and Wales.

At the same time, there were growing industrial relations problems, with the uniformed prison staff in open dispute with governors, with headquarters and with the government over work conditions and pay.

The mid- to late 1980s, however, marked a turning point in Scotland's prisons. The government negotiated new conditions of service and pay with prison staff. Significantly, there was a response from within the SPS itself. There has been a wide-ranging and fundamental review of prisons which has led to the espousal of a new 'vision' of the nature of imprisonment and of what prisons are seen as offering both to the prisoners and to society at large.

The results of this review, especially as they affect the prison regime, are contained in a very important document published in 1990, *Opportunity and Responsibility: Developing New Approaches to the Management of the Long-Term Prison System in Scotland* (1990). This document expounds a view of the purposes of imprisonment which informs the new mission statement for the

Service. At the heart of this new approach are the interconnected ideas of the 'responsible' prisoner and of the prison as delivering services to a range of client groups.

The idea of the responsible prisoner is that inmates should be treated as rational individuals who have knowingly broken the law and are, as a consequence, being punished for it. The purpose of the prison, it is argued, is to create the conditions for the prisoner to reflect upon his or her crime and to make a positive choice not to offend again. The role of the prison is to supply opportunities and services, including positive regimes, which may help in this, but not to force prisoners to make use of them. Rather, the prison should hold prisoners in humane conditions which guarantee the safety of the public but which are not in themselves deliberately or unnecessarily oppressive.

Opportunity and Responsibility is an important document. It is a genuine attempt on the part of the SPS to evolve a coherent philosophy of the purposes of imprisonment and the nature of a modern prison regime. It is, however, but one product of a series of changes that have taken place in the SPS in the late 1980s and the early 1990s.

The plan for change was set out in a paper published by the SPS in 1989, *Business Plan 1989–92*. This paper began with a 'mission statement', identifying the management tasks, explaining the corporate philosophy of the service and identifying priority areas. Priority areas listed were: effective and efficient management; improved training for staff; the development of constructive regimes for inmates which foster self-respect, help maintain family ties and which encourage prisoners to contribute positively to society; the improvement of operational effectiveness; and the delivery of administrative justice in all aspects of the work of the service (pp. 1–4).

One important aspect of this corporate approach was the wish to develop social work services as part of those made generally available to prisoners. This development was closely related to the National Objectives and Standards for Social Work in the Criminal Justice System, the spirit of which, in a prison context, was well captured by the idea of 'Continuity Through Cooperation', the title of a document jointly published by the Social Work Services Group of the Scottish Office and the SPS in 1990. The aim of the document was to set out a framework within which the services of social workers in prisons may be better and more effectively integrated into the prison and also with community-based services for prisoners following release. The revised National Standards on Throughcare now include standards for social work in prisons.

In April 1993 the SPS became an executive agency. Agency status is about specifying clearly and publicly the tasks and responsibilities of the SPS and the levels of service it is expected to deliver. It is designed to make the Service more openly accountable for its performance to the Secretary of State for Scotland, who delegated to the chief executive, through the Agency Framework Document published on 1 April, the authority and flexibility to manage the Service in the way that will best meet the needs of those it serves and provide value for money. The first Corporate Plan for the new agency was published in August 1993. The mission statement of the Service was set out as: 'to keep in custody those committed by the courts; to maintain good order in each prison; to care for prisoners with humanity; and to provide prisoners with a range of opportunities to exercise personal responsibility and to prepare for release'. Five key objectives were also stated: 'to operate a safe and secure service; to be responsive to the needs of those it serves; to deliver quality of service and value for money within available resources; to present prisoners with a range of opportunities to allow them to use their time in prison responsibly; and to strive to fulfil the Citizen's Charter principles in all aspects of its operation' (Corporate Plan, 1993: pp. 7–8).

In June 1995 a new Corporate Plan was published which describes the progress the SPS has made since it was given agency status and also sets goals and objectives to be achieved over the next period until 1998. The aims and objectives as set out are a continuation of those proposed in the earlier corporate plans, and there are listed also a number of key performance measures and targets. Eight measures are mentioned, ranging from the number of prisoners unlawfully at large, improving the basic quality of life for inmates, and containing the average costs per prison place, to controlling the number of serious assaults on staff and inmates.

These documents, all produced in the period from 1988 to 1995, can be seen as part of a sustained effort to conceive of the SPS in a realistic and positive light. Further changes are planned to improve the quality of prison regimes and to reduce costs, but the secure accommodation of prisoners continues to be the principal aim of the Service. The Corporate Plan (1995) notes projections of the rise in the prison population over the next three years and observes that the planned expansion in the prison estate will not be sufficient to meet these projections. The use of the Private Finance Initiative is therefore being considered for the design, construction, management and finance of a new prison to provide accommodation for 500 prisoners. The population projections are: 1995–6, 5,750; 1996–7, 5,900; 1997–8, 6,100.

The Structure of the Prison Population

This section will describe the structure of the population inside Scotland's prisons.

Figure 8.1 shows the average daily population in all penal establishments between 1950 and 1994. As can be seen, the graph

Figure 8.1   The   average   daily   population   in   penal establishments, 1950–94.

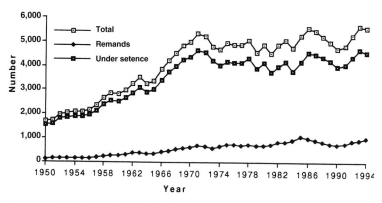

Source: Prison Statistics Scotland

records three lines: the total average daily population, the average daily population under sentence, and the average daily population on remand. The average daily population records those offenders in custody counted at a certain time of day (those prisoners on home leave at the time are counted as they are still serving a period of imprisonment).

The line for the total average daily population shows a steady if somewhat irregular rise over the period to 1970. The population starts at about 1,800 in 1950 and finishes at approximately 5,600 in 1994. It can be seen that there are two periods of rapid increase: a first phase between 1950 and the early 1960s, followed by a short-lived decline, before the line begins its second phase of rapid increase from the mid-1960s to the early 1970s. Thereafter, the line becomes more irregular in shape with noticeable downturns and upswings, which indicates a fluctuating prison population. In relative terms, however, it is to be noted that the period between 1970 and 1994 is one in which the total average daily population does not significantly increase. It must be noted,

125

however, that since 1990 the population in penal establishments has been rising significantly and in 1994 stood at 5,585.

The irregularity of the line after 1970 appears to be accounted for by swings in the average daily population under sentence. This can be seen by comparing the two lines for remand and under sentence and by noting the proportion of the prison population which the graph shows to be composed of those under sentence. The line for those under remand does show a steady increase over the period. The line for those under sentence is uneven and follows in shape the line for the total population. As the population under sentence must reflect the custodial sentencing pattern of the criminal courts, it can be concluded that the irregularity of the lines shown here is picking up on yearly differences in the number of custodial sentences passed by the courts.

One factor which has affected the prison population since 1993 was the impact of the Prisoner and Criminal Proceedings (Scotland) Act 1993. This Act changed the rules relating to early release for prisoners serving less than four years. Instead of being released automatically after serving two-thirds of their sentence, prisoners are now released after serving one-half (effective on those sentenced on or after 1 October 1993). The transitional arrangements made for early release, set out in this Act, resulted in a decrease of 600 in the number of short-term prisoners on 1 October 1993: the population decreased immediately from 5,800 to 5,200. Direct comparisons of the figures for 1993 and subsequent years with those for any previous years must therefore be treated with caution.

Since 1987, the number of young offenders sent to YOIs has fallen. In 1987, the total average daily population in YOIs was 987, but this had decreased to 720 by 1994; it reached a low point in 1991 of 684. Since 1991, the young offender population has, however, followed the same pattern as the adult population. In 1985, remand prisoners formed 21 per cent of the total average daily population and since then they have accounted for between 16 per cent and 18 per cent.

Receptions into Penal Establishments, 1980–94

The average daily population reflects only the average 'lock-up' figure each night. It gives no measure of the flow into and through the system. Another measure known as 'receptions' is, however, available and is useful in this context. A reception is counted when one (or more) warrants from a court arrives for an individual at a penal establishment on the same day. The individual may already be serving a sentence and a further custodial sentence is imposed; this is also counted as a reception. Thus, receptions are not equivalent to 'persons received' but they do provide a measure of 'flow'. Figure 8.2 shows the receptions into penal establishments for the period 1980–94.

Figure 8.2   Receptions into penal establishments, 1980–94.

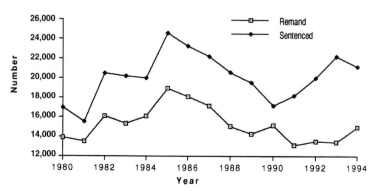

Source: Prison Statistics Scotland.

Figure 8.2 also shows the number of remand and sentenced receptions and the trends in such receptions. It can be seen that the two lines follow the same broad pattern during most of the period, but begin to diverge after 1989. The high point for both was in 1985. Thereafter, the curve for receptions under sentence begins to fall steadily until 1990, after which it begins to rise. In 1992, 22,157 prisoners were received under sentence, but this had fallen by 5 per cent to 21,111 in 1994. The line for receptions on remand has fallen steadily from a high point in 1985. The total number of receptions on remand stood at 14,922 in 1994. This is an 11 per cent increase over the 1993 figure (13,412).

Receptions of Fine Defaulters into Penal Establishments

One of the long-term problems of the Scottish prison system has been the high proportion of fine defaulters who are imprisoned. Figure 8.3 records the percentage of fine default receptions between 1950 and 1994.

As can be seen, the line shows a steadily upward, if somewhat erratic, trend. It shows a rise in the percentage of fine default receptions from about 30 per cent in 1950 to a high point in 1987 of 50 per cent of all receptions under sentence. For a good deal of the period, it can be seen that fine defaulters composed over 40 per cent of all receptions under sentence. This figure is reached first in the early 1960s and only falls below this for a few years in that decade. Otherwise, the line exceeds the 40 per cent mark for the remaining 20 years, although, as was said, the line does fluctuate. It dips violently from 1989 to 1990, then rises until 1991, where it has remained (except for a dip in 1992). In 1994, there were a total of 8,875 fine default receptions, an 8 per cent decrease on 1993. This yearly fluctuation confirms the erratic nature of imprisonment for fine default.

Figure 8.3   Fine defaulters expressed as a percentage of total receptions, 1950–94.

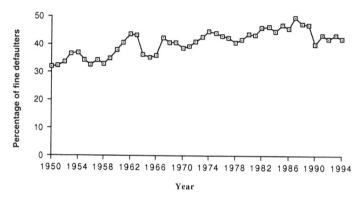

Source: Prison Statistics Scotland.

By international standards, these are very high figures. They indicate that over 40 per cent of those sent to penal establishments each year in Scotland are not imprisoned for the crime or offence they committed originally, but for not paying their fines. As a fraction of the total prison population, the number of receptions of fine defaulters is about 80–100 per day. The introduction of the supervised attendance order in 1991 is a recognition of the seriousness of this problem and clearly shows that the government intends to try and resolve the problem.

The Demographic Structure of the Prison Population

This brief section will examine the age and gender characteristics of the imprisoned population in 1994.

It will be remembered that penal establishments are divided into two principal types: those for adults and those for young offenders between the ages of 16 and 21. In 1994, the average daily population in all penal establishments was 5,585; 5,408 of these were males and 177 or 3 per cent were females.

129

The adult population accounted for 3,785 or 83 per cent of those under sentence in 1994, and young offenders accounted for 720 or 16 per cent. The remaining numbers in 1994 were composed of those recalled from a supervision order such as parole (37), others (28), persons sentenced by a court martial (21) and civil prisoners (1), which accounted for 1 per cent of all persons under sentence.

It is possible to provide figures for direct receptions (that is, excluding fine default receptions) by age groups. These are interesting because they show the age groups most likely to be sent to a penal establishment.

In 1994 there were 12,200 direct receptions. Of these, 2,852 were composed of the 16–20 age group and 6,378 were accounted for by the 21–30 age group. Thereafter, the number of receptions for the other age groups decline: there were 2,008 in the 31–40 age group, 652 for the 41–50 age group and only 310 for the over-50 age group. If the first two age groups are combined (16–30), then together they account for 76 per cent of all direct receptions. The presence of the 16–30 age group in the number of receptions has been on the increase since 1979.

The Criminal Record of Offenders in Penal Establishments

In 1994, 79 per cent of direct receptions into penal establishments had a previous custodial sentence; 11 per cent had a previous non-custodial sentence; only 10 per cent were reported as having no sentence of any type before. These figures show that the majority of prisoners are repeat offenders who have already had experience of custodial sentences.

As was seen in earlier chapters, custodial sentences are used more for some crimes and offences than for others. In 1994, there were 12,200 direct receptions for all crimes and offences; 5,985 or 49 per cent were for crimes of dishonesty. Within this group, the greatest number of receptions were for other thefts (2,285) and housebreaking (1,799). Direct receptions for crimes of violence comprised 1,266 or 10 per cent of the total direct receptions for all crimes and offences. Within this group, the most common number of receptions were for serious assault (623) and robbery (399).

With regard to offences (rather than crimes), there were 3,424 direct receptions in that year. Most of these were for breach of the peace, which accounted for 1,570 or 45 per cent of all direct receptions for offences. Only 922 receptions were for motor vehicle offences, the majority of these (723 or 78 per cent) being for unlawful use of a vehicle.

The Length of Sentence Imposed

This section will examine the length of sentence imposed in relation to adult and young offender direct receptions in 1994.

In 1994, there were 9,349 adult direct receptions. Of these, 5,653 or 60 per cent were for sentences of six months or less. Within this band, there were three peaks: sentences of 60 days or two months accounting for 1,088 or 19 per cent; sentences of 90 days or three months accounting for 2,203 or 39 per cent; and sentences between three months and six months accounting for 1,546 or 27 per cent.

There were 3,696 receptions for sentences over six months and up to and including life sentences. Most of these receptions were in the six months and less than two years category totalling 2,859 or 77 per cent. There were 444 (12 per cent) receptions for two years and less than four years and 368 (10 per cent) for four years, and over, excluding life. There were 25 receptions for life sentences (1 per cent). If life sentences are excluded then the average sentence imposed was 268 days. This figure is heavily biased by the small number of very long sentences given.

131

The average sentence imposed on young offenders sent to YOIs was 251 days in 1994. There were 2,855 direct receptions of which 1,653 were for less than six months; 1,190 were for sentences of six months to life. There were 12 life sentences.

It is possible to provide figures for the percentage of direct receptions by crime and offence category and length of sentence imposed. As one would expect, the greatest percentage of long sentences were given for the more serious crimes. For example, 75 per cent of sentences for robbery were for 18 months and over; in serious assault and attempted murder, 43 per cent were for the same period. In drug offences, 38 per cent of sentences were for 18 months and over. By contrast, only 2 per cent of sentences for unlawful use of a motor vehicle were for 18 months or over.

The average sentence imposed for robbery was 1,186 days; this is the longest average sentence for any of the crimes excluding the homicides. It is followed by serious assault and attempted murder (742 days), drugs offences (578 days) and fraud (231 days). The next highest average sentence is for housebreaking, at 210 days.

International Comparisons

It is always useful to view the use of imprisonment in an international perspective. Statistics are published by several agencies which allow this to be done, but, as with all statistical comparisons, one must interpret the figures with care and in context. In Figure 8.4, the figures provided by the Council of Europe are calculated by gathering returns from each member state and then presenting them in a table. This is complicated by the fact that different member states calculate their figures in different ways. Nevertheless, these figures provide a starting point for analysis. They have been combined with extracts from tables produced by the Canadian Correctional Services. In all cases, figures are presented as a rate per 100,000 of the adult inhabitants in each country.

Figure 8.4   Detention rate per 100,000 inhabitants for selected countries

United States of America	529
Canada	120
Scotland	115
Austria	91
England and Wales	89
Italy	89
France	86
Germany	81
Netherlands	51

As can be seen, the USA has by far the highest rate of detention per 100,000 inhabitants, followed by Canada. It is noticeable, however, that Scotland has the highest of any of the Council of Europe countries. Strictly speaking, the Scottish figure is exceeded in 1994 by that of Northern Ireland but this figure is often excluded from these comparisons owing to the very special circumstances which prevail there.

Early Release

Until the Prisoners and Criminal Proceedings (Scotland) Act 1993, which was enacted on 29 March 1993, all prisoners serving sentences of a fixed length were entitled to remission of one-third of sentence. Remission could be forfeited for disciplinary offences but once a prisoner was released with remission, the outstanding period of the sentence was effectively cancelled. In addition, prisoners serving sentences over a certain length (18 months) were entitled to be considered for release on parole licence before their remission date. The 1993 Act abolished the concept of remission in favour of a system of early release entitlements and restricted the availability of parole to prisoners serving sentences of four years or more.

Under the new arrangements, all prisoners who are serving under four years are released unconditionally at half sentence, subject to any added days owing to misconduct during their prison sentence. Those prisoners who are serving sentences of four years or more are released on licence at two-thirds of the sentence if parole has not been granted already. Again, this is subject to added days attributable to misconduct.

All prisoners sentenced on or after 1 October 1993 are liable to be returned to prison if they are convicted of a further offence punishable by imprisonment committed after release but before the expiry of the full term of the sentence. Adults will be subject to post-release supervision if they are serving sentences of four years or more. For those serving less than four years there is no compulsory post-release supervision unless the court imposes a supervised release order where it considers that the offender poses a serious risk. This provision is only available for sentences of over 12 months.

Parole

Parole is a form of early release from the prison on licence. There is no right to parole, and recommendations governing its application are made by the Parole Board for Scotland. Prisoners serving mandatory life sentences may be released by the Secretary of State on licence if the Parole Board so recommends and after consulting the judiciary.

All prisoners on determinate sentences of four years or more are eligible for parole after serving half of their sentence. Supervision on release is compulsory for those serving sentences of four years or more and for those serving lesser sentences if the court considers it necessary. The duration of the licence is potentially for the full period of the sentence, and all licences will be liable to be recalled on the recommendation of the Parole Board if prisoners breach their licence conditions. For those serving discretionary life sentences, that is a life sentence imposed by the court for a crime other than murder, the court will specify a period after which the prisoner will be entitled to have his or her case referred to the Parole Board. The Parole Board will have the power to direct the release of the prisoner.

In considering cases for parole, the Parole Board will have before it reports from prison officers, social workers and other relevant agencies. Research has shown that parole boards pay particular attention to such factors as the likely risk of reoffending, the prisoner's response to imprisonment, and the social and familial conditions that will await the prisoner on release. The central task of the Parole Board is to assess the risk of the offender committing offences while on a parole licence.

Conclusion

This chapter has tried to present a balanced overview of the Scottish prison system. If the figures presented are summarised, then they provide a description of a typical individual who is received into prison: this would be a young man, under 30 years of age, who has been imprisoned for a short time (under six months) for a crime of dishonesty; also, many of those received into penal establishments will be fine defaulters. In reality, with the exception of the large number of fine defaulters, this is a fairly typical description of those who are received into a prison in any European country.

Chapter 9

◆

Juvenile Justice and the
Children's Hearings System

So far, in this book, the focus has been on either young or adult offenders. In this chapter, it will shift to an examination of the way in which juvenile offenders are dealt with in Scotland (juvenile offenders are defined as those who are aged between 8 and 15 inclusive). Scotland has a unique system of juvenile justice known as the Children's Hearings. The Children's Hearing or panel is unique in several respects. First, it is not a court of law which sets out to establish the question of innocence or guilt, but a tribunal whose aim is to assess the needs of children who have committed offences or who may for other reasons be in need of compulsory measures of care or protection. The operation of hearings is subject to oversight by the Scottish Committee of the Council on Tribunals. Second, it is composed of ordinary members of the public who volunteer to undertake the duties associated with serving on the panel, as it is known. Third, it is an example of what criminologists call 'decriminalisation', that is, a way of responding to crime which emphasises non-penal means. The Children's Hearing, therefore, cannot sentence those who come before it for breaking the law to any penal sanctions; rather, the hearings decide on compulsory measures of care for a child, and it is the duty of local authorities to discharge their decision.

The Children's Hearing is, in many ways, a radical institution which has attracted a considerable amount of international attention. The purpose of this chapter is to describe the Children's Hearing system by looking briefly at how it has developed, how it operates and at the decisions it makes.

While the Children's Hearings system is the cornerstone of the juvenile justice system in Scotland, it is not the only means available to deal with juveniles who commit criminal offences. Juveniles who commit serious crimes, such as robbery, rape or murder, will be dealt with by the criminal courts, including the High Court. In certain circumstances, the criminal courts will remit a case to the Hearing, while in others, such as a murder, the courts will dispose of cases themselves. The character of the relationship between the Hearings system and the criminal courts was established at the time of the introduction of the former and will be described below.

In the last few years, the government has undertaken a thorough review of the role of the Children's Hearing system and of its relationship with the other agencies involved in child care, including the criminal courts. The results of this review were announced in the White Paper, *Scotland's Children: Proposals for Child Care Policy and Law* (1993). The White Paper contains a number of proposals that affect the workings of the Children's Hearing system. These proposals have been legislated for in two recent acts of parliament, the Local Government etc. (Scotland) Act 1994 and the Children (Scotland) Act 1995. This chapter will describe these new measures which have been introduced by this legislation. The primary aim of these measures is to strengthen the operation of the Hearing system. The legislation also introduces a new body, The Scottish Children's Reporter Administration, and a new official, The Principal Reporter. There are also new measures introduced for the protection of children.

Background to the Children's Hearing

The Children's Hearings system was established by the Social Work (Scotland) Act 1968. It came into operation on 15 April 1971 when it took over responsibility from the courts for dealing with most juveniles. The ideas lying behind the Children's Hearing were recommended by the Kilbrandon Committee which was an inquiry set up by the government to examine, among other things, the question of young people and their relationship to the criminal justice system. The Kilbrandon Committee reported in 1964. In its report, the Committee argued that the issue of juvenile offending needed to be considered in a broad context; it suggested that offending was but one aspect of a deeper, underlying social and psychological malaise that could also manifest itself in other kinds of troublesome behaviour. The Committee thus proposed that juvenile offending ought to be seen in essentially the same light as all other behaviour that indicated that a child 'had gone off the rails'. The Committee drew no distinction between child offenders and children in need of care and protection in relation to compulsory measures of care.

This analysis led the Committee to suggest that the then existing juvenile courts were unsuited to dealing with the problem. This was because the juvenile court tried to combine two roles which the Kilbrandon Committee felt were better separated: the obligation to look after the welfare and interests of the child and also to serve as a court of law within a criminal justice context. The Committee argued that these roles pulled in different directions and thus could well come into conflict with one another.

The innovative nature of the Kilbrandon proposals lay in the sharpness with which it distinguished between treatment and criminal justice. The recommendation, therefore, was to separate the two and to make the Children's Hearings responsible for the welfare and interests of the child. The original proposal of the Committee was that the Children's Hearings should become part of the educational services organised by local authorities. This specific recommendation was not accepted and the Hearing system became the joint responsibility of the Secretary of State and local authorities: under the 1968 Act, the Secretary of State appoints members and finances their training, whereas local authorities provide facilities and pay expenses of members and at the same time (up to 31 March 1996) employ the reporters.

The second recommendation of the Kilbrandon Committee was that the body responsible for dispensing treatment, the Panel, ought to be composed not of experts but of ordinary members of the public. The only qualification for membership was that these individuals ought to have experience of, and interest in, children and their families and be sympathetic enough to be able to communicate with them. The Committee envisaged that members of the Panel would come from as wide a range of social backgrounds as possible so as to be able to understand the social situations of the children who came before them.

The Kilbrandon Committee made two other important recommendations. It proposed that the administration of the new Hearings system should be the responsibility of a new official, the Reporter. It recommended also that it should be possible for any individual or organisation to refer a child to the Hearings system.

The Operation of the Children's Hearing

The Reporter

The Reporter has a duty to investigate all reports or referrals before making a decision on what action to take in the interests of the child. The Reporter has two tasks. In the case of an alleged offence, the Reporter has to decide if there is sufficient evidence to establish a prima facie case in law. Secondly, the Reporter has to decide whether the evidence justifies the possible use of compulsory measures of care.

The Reporter has discretion to decide the next stage of action. This will first be an initial investigation in which the Reporter calls for reports from social workers and other relevant individuals who know the child or the circumstances which gave rise to the referral. After the initial investigation the Reporter has three choices:

1. The Reporter may decide that no further action is required. The child and parents are informed of this but it is not unusual for the Reporter to do this in person and to warn the child about his or her future behaviour.

2. The Reporter may refer the child to the local authority for informal advice and guidance by the social work department.

3. The Reporter may decide to bring the child before a Children's Hearing because, in the Reporter's view, the child is in need of compulsory measures of care. If the Reporter decides to refer the child to the Hearing for possible measures of compulsory care, then the Reporter must state in writing the grounds of the referral.

It can be seen that the Reporter is a key part of the Children's Hearing system. The Kilbrandon Committee did not propose any special qualification for those who wished to become Reporters other than that they were to possess a good education and, most importantly, to have an interest in the welfare of children. As the Children's Hearing system has developed, it has become clear that the position of Reporter requires great skill and knowledge, and an emphasis is increasingly being placed on training.

The plans for the reorganisation of local government in Scotland will not affect the duties carried out by Reporters, but will have an effect on their relationship with local authorities. The Local Government etc. (Scotland) Act 1994 abolished the Regional Councils which are presently responsible for the Children's Hearing system, including Reporters' departments. In the new structure to local government, there will be many more unitary authorities, some of which would have had very small Reporters' departments as a consequence. Against this background, the government has decided to create a new central service called the Scottish Children's Hearing Reporter Administration, with a chief officer called the Principal Reporter. The Principal Reporter has the ultimate responsibility for the decisions of Reporters. Reporters will, however, still operate at the local level and will retain a maximum devolved responsibility for decision-making and for working closely with the local Children's Panels.

The Children's Panel

The requirement to have a Children's Panel and to establish a Children's Panel Advisory Committee was established by the 1968 Act and carried forward by the Local Government etc. (Scotland) Act 1994. The duty of this Committee will be to submit names of possible panel members to the Secretary of State who has the responsibility for the appointment of members of the panel. It will be possible for two or more unitary authorities to set up Joint Advisory Committees, if the Secretary of State agrees to this, or for the Secretary of State to require two or more authorities to form Joint Advisory Committees. The responsibility for the training of panel members will be the Secretary of State's and the unitary authority's.

Each Children's Hearing will be composed of individuals whose names are on the lists nominated by the Advisory Committee and approved of by the Secretary of State. A Hearing will consist of three members, one of whom acts as chairman; the Hearing shall not consist of solely male or female members. The responsibility of the Hearing is to consider cases referred to it by the Reporter, and to make decisions as to what compulsory measures of care (or other permissible action) are, in its view, required in the best interests of each child.

The Grounds of Referral

The grounds on which the Reporter may make a referral to a Children's Hearing are set out in the 1968 Act and in the Children (Scotland) Act 1995. These grounds are complex but set out to capture the wide-ranging view the Kilbrandon Committee took of the nature of adolescent problems and thus are not confined only to describing behaviour which breaks the criminal law. Generally, the grounds can be divided into two types: offence referrals and non-offence referrals. As will be seen, most referrals are for offences, although in recent years non-offence referrals have increased as a proportion of the total.

Offence referrals are those which relate to the commission of actual offences. Some non-offence referrals may be in respect of a child who is thought to be at risk of committing an offence by, for instance, being beyond the control of parents or falling into bad associations. Children may also be referred to the Hearing if they are in moral danger or are the victims of particular types of crimes, such as incest.

In more detail the grounds for referral, as set out in the 1995 Act, are when the child:

1. is beyond the control of his or her parents or any relevant person;

2. is falling into bad association or is exposed to moral danger;

3. is likely to suffer unnecessarily or be impaired seriously in his or her health owing to lack of parental care;

4. is a child in respect of whom any of the offences mentioned in Schedule 1 of the Criminal Procedure (Scotland) Act 1975 has been committed;

5. is, or is likely to become, a member of the same household as a child in respect of whom any of the offences referred to in paragraph 4 above has been committed;

6. is, or is likely to become, a member of the same household as a person who has committed any of the offences referred to in paragraph 4 above;

7. is, or is likely to become, a member of the same household as a person in respect of whom an offence under section 2A to 2C of the Sexual Offences (Scotland) Act 1976 (incest and intercourse with a child by step-parent or person in position of trust) has been committed by a member of that household;

8. has failed to attend school regularly without reasonable excuse;

9. has committed an offence;

10. has misused alcohol or any drug, whether or not a controlled drug, within the meaning of the Misuse of Drugs Act 1971;

11. has misused a volatile substance by deliberately inhaling its vapour, other than for medicinal purposes;

12. is being provided with accommodation by the local authority because the child appears to have no responsible adult to care for him or her, or is the subject of a parental responsibility order which has transferred parental rights to a local authority.

The offences referred to in paragraphs 4–6 of Schedule 1 of the 1975 Criminal Procedure (Scotland) Act include offences such as child neglect, sexual or other abuse, incest and other sexual offences.

The Hearing

The Hearing is the body of lay members who make the decisions on what to do with children once they have been referred by the Reporter. Attendance at the Hearing is normally compulsory for both the child and the parents; the parents can be fined if they fail to attend. Before a Hearing can proceed, it is necessary for the parents and the child to accept the grounds of the referral as they have been stated by the Reporter. If the child or parents do not accept the grounds, the Hearing can either discharge the referral or make an application to the sheriff for a finding as to whether the grounds are established. If the sheriff finds that the grounds have been established, the case is returned to the Hearing for disposal or, under new arrangements introduced by the 1995 Act, the sheriff can dispose of the case.

The Hearing is held in private, with only the Panel members, the child and its parents, the Reporter and other relevant persons such as social workers present. As the Hearing is not a court of law, there will be no prosecution or defence agents there, although both the child and parents can have a representative present if they wish. The press is allowed to attend a Hearing but cannot identify the child in any subsequent report.

The layout of the Hearing is designed to be informal. The Panel members sit round a table with the child and its family and decide in the light of the discussion whether compulsory measures of care are necessary.

The task of the Hearing is to reach a decision on what the best interests of the child are and how these can be secured by any action that the Hearing can take. To enable it to make its decisions the Hearing will normally receive reports on the child and the family from social workers, teachers, psychiatrists and other relevant individuals. These reports are discussed with the child and parents; indeed, the Panel has the responsibility to involve the family in the discussion and the decision-making as much as it can practically manage.

Safeguarders

Safeguarders were introduced by the 1975 Children Act under Section 43A of the 1968 Act. Their role is to safeguard the interests of the child in cases before the Children's Hearings or the sheriff court where there is or may be a conflict between the interests of the child and those of its parents. The Children (Scotland) Act enhances the position of the safeguarder, whose role it is to prepare reports which put an independent view to the Hearing or to attend the sheriff court. Safeguarders, are appointed either by the Hearing or by the sheriff.

The Decisions

The Panel can reach a number of decisions: it can decide that no further action needs to be taken or it can determine that the child is in need of compulsory care of one sort or another. There are two types of compulsory care both of which impose supervision requirements. The child can be placed under a non-residential supervision requirement in the community, which means that the child will remain in the family home or a foster home but under the supervision of a social worker. Section 44(1)(a) of the 1968 Social Work (Scotland) Act requires the child to 'submit to supervision in accordance with such conditions as they [the Hearing] may impose'. These conditions are designed to be positive and can include residing in an approved place other than the parental home, for example with a relative or with foster parents. Alternatively, under Section 44(1)(b) of the Act, the child may, under a residential supervision requirement, be removed from the family home and placed in a local authority home or residential school.

Supervision requirements last for one year and lapse at that point unless they have been reviewed. Normally, all supervision requirements are reviewed at the end of the year at a review meeting of the Hearing where the child and parents will be present. The Panel can decide to terminate the requirements or to extend them for another period. Review meetings can be held at the request of the parents or child after three months or after six months if the requirements are a continuation of previous ones. The aim of the 1968 Act was, rather than imposing set time limits on the duration of supervision, to leave room for flexibility. The Act requires that a child shall not 'be subject to a supervision requirement for any longer than is in his interest', and this is why supervision requirements are regularly reviewed. The 1995 Children (Scotland) Act, however, empowers the Hearing to state a definite period after which a review will take place. The aim is to give the Hearing an opportunity to assess the progress the child has made and to modify the supervision requirement if that is thought necessary. A supervision requirement ceases to have effect when the child attains the age of 18.

Place of Safety Orders

The Children's Hearing system deals with children who may be in need of care and protection as well as children who have offended. The proportion of care and protection referrals to total referrals has changed markedly over the 1980s and 1990s and now represents 43 per cent, which includes the most complex and most difficult cases to handle. Children who are considered to be in special or acute need of protection can be removed from home or other places to a place of safety by means other than a residential supervision requirement: the Children (Scotland) Act 1995 introduced the child protection order. This order replaces the authorisation in the 1968 Act to remove a child to a place of safety.

The Child Protection Order

While the child protection order involves the Reporter and the Hearing, it also involves the courts, especially the sheriff court, in that it is the sheriff court, rather than the Hearing, which is empowered to make an order. The aim of the order is to allow the authorities to place a child temporarily in an approved establishment for its protection and safety. The use of the order is not restricted to circumstances in which a child is alleged to have committed an offence but can be used also when a child is believed to be in moral danger or out of the control of parents.

The background to the child protection order is the recommendation made by Lord Clyde in his *Inquiry into the Removal of Children from Orkney*, published in 1991. Lord Clyde recognised the need for a means to remove children to a place of safety but concluded that the existing legislation allowed for excessive discretion about the circumstances in which removal can be sought. The child protection order will allow the removal of a child only where there is reasonable cause to believe that the child is likely to suffer significant harm and where immediate removal to a place of safety is necessary for the child's protection.

The child protection order can only be granted by a sheriff on an application by a local authority, the police or any individual. The application will have to be accompanied by such information as the sheriff requires. A Justice of the Peace will be able to grant an order if a sheriff is not available, but the order will then have to be confirmed within 24 hours. An order which is not used within three days will lapse.

The parents and the child will be able to appeal to the sheriff against a child protection order or to request a variation in its conditions. The Reporter is empowered to discharge an order where he or she considers that the criteria for the order are no longer met. Also, the Reporter will be responsible for calling an early meeting of a Hearing (usually within the first day) to consider the welfare of the child. This Hearing will also consider the need for a short extension of the order so that a second Hearing can consider the grounds for referral.

Exclusion Orders

The Children (Scotland) Act 1995 also introduces another order aimed at excluding abusers from the home. An exclusion order will only be granted by a sheriff on an application. The stated aim of the order is to save a child from significant harm, and it should be noted that there is no presumption of sexual abuse.

Assessment Orders

An assessment order has been introduced by the 1995 Act. The aim of this order is to provide social workers with a means of gaining access to a child to assess its safety when the parents refuse to co-operate. The order will be granted only on application to a sheriff. The order will be granted only if there is reasonable cause to suspect that the child is suffering significant harm and that an assessment is necessary to resolve these concerns. The order can extend up to seven days and will specify the nature of the assessment.

The Criminal Courts

The criminal courts can be involved with juveniles at three stages. First, there are some very serious offences, such as murder, sexual assaults and some property crimes, which will be directed to the courts by the procurator fiscal after receiving a report from the police. The court can then dispose of the case by the normal procedures or it can refer the case to the Children's Hearing for advice or to be dealt with by the Hearing altogether.

Second, as was described, the sheriff court can become involved if the child or its parents reject or challenge the grounds of the referral as set out by the Reporter. In these circumstances, the sheriff will make a decision as to whether the grounds have been established. If the sheriff affirms the grounds, the case is returned to the Hearing or disposed of by the sheriff; if the sheriff rejects the grounds set out by the Reporter, the case is dismissed and no further action is possible.

Third, any appeals against the decision of a Hearing will be heard by a sheriff. There are two grounds on which an appeal may be made. The first is alleged irregularities in procedure, such as a failure to notify the parents of the date of a Hearing or of the Hearing to state reasons for its decision. The other ground is an appeal against the decision itself: for example, the child or the parents may not agree that supervision is necessary or that the residential home to which a child is to be sent is a suitable one. Finally, the Court of Session may become involved if a further appeal on a point of law is made against the decision of the sheriff.

The Children's Hearing at Work

This section examines the number of referrals to the Children's Hearing, the types of case with which it deals and the decisions made.

Figure 9.1 shows the number of referrals to Reporters from 1972 to 1994. As can be seen, there has been a steady rise in the number of referrals from about 24,219 in 1972 to 42,924 in 1994. The curve describing the referrals is a little erratic, with an

Figure 9.1 Referrals to Reporters and number of children involved, 1972–94.

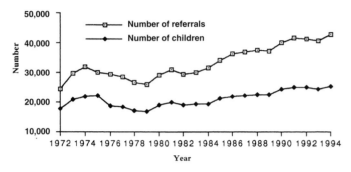

Source: Referrals of Children to Reporters and Children's Hearings.

initial rise in the first two years followed by a fall in the next five to 1979. Thereafter, the curve begins to rise again until 1981, when it falls once again, but only for one year. The remainder of the period is marked by a constant but gradual increase in numbers that is somewhat slower than the rise in the first years from 1972 to 1974. The number of referrals has, however, fallen slightly from 1991 when there were 41,560 to 1993 when there were 40,503. There has been an overall increase in referrals of 77 per cent.

If the number of children referred is examined, then a slightly different pattern emerges. In 1972, 17,950 children were referred; by 1994 the number had risen to 25,232 – an increase of 41 per cent. If, however, the number of children referred is expressed per 1,000 of the population under 16 years of age, then there has been an increase from 12 per 1,000 to 24 per 1,000; this is an increase of 100 per cent. The highest rate of referral was in 1992 when 24.3 per 1,000 were referred.

A greater number of boys than girls are referred. In 1972, the number of boys referred per 1,000 of the population under 16 was 20; this had risen to 30 by 1994. In comparison, the figures for girls were about 4 in 1972 and 18 in 1994, and this continues the upward trend. The number of referrals varies with age. The peak age for all referrals is 15, with offence referrals exceeding non-offence referrals by more than 2:1 in 1994.

Grounds of Referrals

In this section the grounds of referrals recorded by Reporters between 1972 and 1994 will be examined.

Figure 9.2 shows the decline in offence referrals to Reporters between 1972 and 1994. As can be seen, offence referrals still remain the most common ground of referral throughout the period but show a significant decrease over the period. There has been a noticeable corresponding increase in non-offence referrals, especially those connected to being the victim of an offence, lack of parental care or being beyond control. The rate of referrals on non-offence grounds exceeded that for offence referrals for the first time in 1993.

Figure 9.2   Offence referrals, 1972–94.

Source: Referrals of Children to Reporters and Children's Hearings.

151

Between 1993 and 1994 there was an increase in referrals on alleged offence grounds for boys of 9 per cent and for girls of 22 per cent. The most common reason for non-offence referrals for boys and girls in 1994 was for being the victim of an offence, followed by lack of parental control.

Action by Reporters

Figure 9.3 shows the changes in initial action taken by Reporters between 1972 and 1994. The most significant change over the period is the decline in the proportion of cases which Reporters refer to the Hearing and the increase in the number of cases in which no action is taken. There has been a slight decrease in the proportion of cases referred to the police juvenile liaison schemes and an increase in the proportion referred to social work departments. In general, these changes seem to indicate that Reporters are now dealing with a greater number of cases by

Figure 9.3   Initial action taken by reporters, 1976–94.

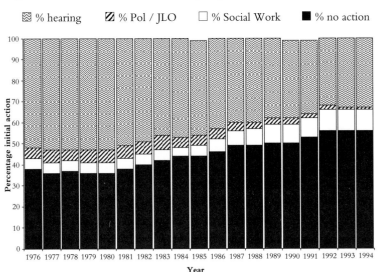

Source: Referrals of Children to Reporters and Children's Hearings.

152

'informal means'. The most significant increase, however, is in the 'no action taken' category; in 1994, 57 per cent of referrals were dealt with in this way.

Children's Hearings in 1994

Figure 9.4 is taken from the annual statistical bulletin *Referrals of Children to Reporters and Children's Hearings 1993* and is a convenient representation of the passage of cases through the system in that year. It illustrates the main sources of referral, the outcome of decisions taken by Reporters, and finally the number of cases referred to the Hearing and the action then taken.

There are several main points that come out of Figure 9.4. The first to note is the main source of referral to the Reporter. As can be seen, the police remain the main source of referral, accounting for 73 per cent, followed by educational and other sources (12 per cent), social work departments (10 per cent) and the procurator fiscal (5 per cent).

Figure 9.4 also shows the significance of the action of the Reporter. The most common initial decision was to take no action (56 per cent). Of the 25,232 children who were referred to the Reporter, 7,514 or 30 per cent actually appeared before a Hearing. It can be seen that more offence and offence-related referrals result in no action being taken than is the case with non-offence referrals. In interpreting these statistics, it is to be remembered that a child can be the subject of more than one referral in a year.

Conclusion

This chapter has provided an overview of the juvenile justice system in Scotland. It has sought to highlight the nature of the Children's Hearing, to describe how the system operates and to point out the new measures that are in the process of being introduced.

Figure 9.4 Representation of the Children's Hearings statistics, 1994.

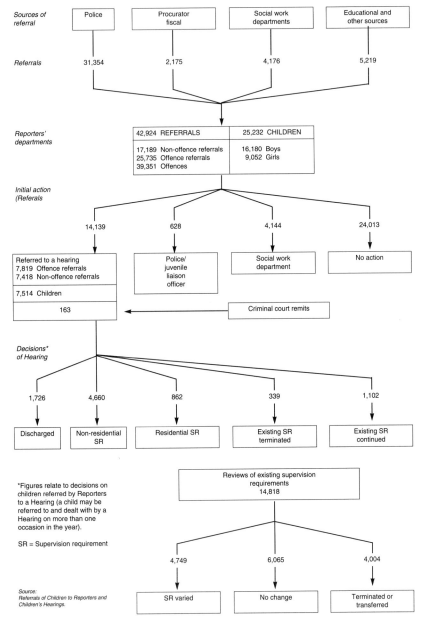

*Figures relate to decisions on children referred by Reporters to a Hearing (a child may be referred to and dealt with by a Hearing on more than one occasion in the year).

SR = Supervision requirement

Source:
Referrals of Children to Reporters and Children's Hearings.

CONCLUSION

The aim of the preceding chapters has been to provide an overview of the Scottish criminal justice process. This task was undertaken primarily because there exists no other readily available descriptive account. The focus has often been on those features which are unique to Scotland and thus lend to its criminal justice process an identity. While this focus is justifiable, it may have created the false impression that the system in Scotland is unlike those elsewhere. This would be unfortunate for two reasons. First, as was said in Chapter 1, the Scottish process belongs to a wider family of legal systems and has much in common with them. Indeed, as was said, the Scottish process may be conceived as a bridge between the Anglo-American common law systems and the civilian systems of continental Europe. Second, it must be remembered that Scotland is part of the UK. Legislation concerning the Scottish process emanates from the UK parliament and, while this legislation must take into account the constitutionally guaranteed independence of the Scottish system, it reflects also the policy concerns of the UK government of the day. As with other areas of legal and social policy, that affecting the criminal justice process is the product, at least in part, of politics and government activity.

These comments raise once more the issue of how the Scottish criminal justice system fits into the wider UK picture. At one level, of course, the answer is clear. Scotland has an independent legal system and, unless the constitutional settlement represented by the Acts of Union of 1707 is changed, this must be, and is, recognised. Legislation affecting the criminal law or criminal procedure of Scotland is, therefore, normally enacted through separate statutes or through separate sections of UK Acts which do not apply, unless it is explicitly stated, to England and Wales and Northern Ireland. At another level, that which is concerned with the policies influencing how, for example, the prisons are to be run or how social work services are to operate, the position is more complex. Here, the study of how criminal justice policy evolves and is put into practice in the two jurisdictions shows interesting differences.

These differences can be shown by examining the background to some of the institutions described earlier – for example, the Children's Hearings system. In both Scotland and England and Wales during the early 1960s, there was a similar concern over how juveniles were dealt with by the criminal justice systems. In many respects, the then existing systems were similar – juveniles were dealt with by modified criminal courts, in Scotland the sheriff court, and in England and Wales the magistrates' court. In both countries there was a considerable criticism of these arrangements and the government reacted by establishing committees in 1964 in both jurisdictions to conduct investigations and to make recommendations. The committee in England and Wales was the Longford Committee and in Scotland it was the Kilbrandon Committee. Although both committees reached a similar conclusion and both recommended explicit welfare responses to the problem of juvenile delinquency, the similarity in the stories ends there. In Scotland the welfare-based proposals were more or less fully implemented in the setting-up of the Children's Hearings system, whereas in England and Wales they became considerably diluted and the end result was a modification of the existing arrangements.

This example shows that even when a common problem is identified, the outcome in the two jurisdictions need not be the same. Other examples can be given. The evolution of policy with regard to the two prison services in the 1980s has differed in important respects. There was no equivalent in England and Wales to the series of papers which culminated in the publication of *Opportunity and Responsibility* (1990) in Scotland. There was the very important Woolf Inquiry into English prisons, which was the report of a committee set up, under the convenorship of Lord Woolf (a judge), in response to the spate of prison disturbances, but this inquiry was imposed on the English prison service. The most important document suggesting fundamental change, in other words, came from outwith the service, not within. Again, and to look at a more specific matter, the policy with regard to how the two prison services react to those prisoners who are HIV positive has differed. The Scottish Prison Service has followed a policy of integrating such prisoners with the general prison population, while this has not been so in England and Wales.

Another area in which policy differs between the two jurisdictions is that related to the delivery of social work services to the criminal justice process. As commentators have noted, one important aim of the Criminal Justice Act 1991 was the promotion of a policy of punishment in the community. This constituted the general framework within which social work services for criminal justice in England and Wales were to be delivered, and this is reflected in the drafting of the National Standards applicable to the probation service. Although, at more or less the same time, the National Standards for Social Work were produced in Scotland, they contained a distinctive policy in several respects. While the Scottish document too encouraged the greater use of community-based sanctions as an alternative to imprisonment, this was not set within a broader framework of a policy of punishment in the community. Rather, the Scottish document, as was seen, was based on certain ideas of what constitutes effective social work intervention into offending behaviour. The result was two documents, promoting the greater use of the same sanctions, but with differing underlying rationales or philosophies.

The point of these examples is not to say that one style of policy is better or worse than another. Rather, the comparisons aim to show that, within broad boundaries, both the evolution of policy and its implementation can be different in Scotland from in England and Wales. These differences are the product of the interaction of a number of factors to which the differences in legal structure are the background. A crucial factor is the devolution of administration. The separate Scottish Office, the separate prison services, the differences in the relationship between social work and criminal justice, the key role of the procurator fiscal, the unique Children's Hearings, all combine to create a distinctive culture in which the institutions of criminal justice in Scotland work. The purpose of this book has been to describe these institutions and this culture.

◆

APPENDIX

Crime and Punishment

In June 1996, the government published a White Paper entitled *Crime and Punishment* which contains proposals for wide-ranging reforms of aspects of the criminal justice and penal process in Scotland. In the Foreword to the White Paper, the Secretary of State for Scotland describes the aim of these proposals as being 'better public protection and providing a more effective and responsive criminal justice system'. The purpose of this Appendix is to provide a summary of the main legislative and other proposals of the White Paper.

The government intends to introduce legislation at an early date to ensure that:

- the current system of summary legal aid is improved
- courts are required to pass a life sentence on an offender convicted for a second time of a serious violent or sexual offence
- offenders are liable to serve in prison the full sentence as handed down by the court
- a small measure of early release can be earned, but only by good behaviour and diligence in prison
- all prisoners serving sentences of 12 months or more are on release subject to standard licence conditions and liable to be recalled to prison if they re-offend

- courts are empowered to order additional post-licence supervision for high-risk offenders, including sex offenders, targeting control at those most likely to be a risk to the public
- the public are better protected against sex offenders through extension of DNA sampling, registration of address and restrictions on employment
- the courts can deal appropriately with mentally disordered offenders
- appeals criteria are revised in the light of the Sutherland Committee recommendations (the government set up in November 1994 the Committee on Appeals Criteria and Alleged Miscarriages of Justice, under the convenorship of Sir Stewart Sutherland; the Committee's report (Cmd 3245) was published on 10 June 1996).

The White Paper contains a number of other proposals which do not require legislation. These proposals include measures to improve the delivery of crime prevention measures and the position of victims in the criminal justice process, approval for the building of a new prison in Scotland at Kilmarnock (to be built under the Private Finance Initiative), and measures to improve the court process and to tackle drug and alcohol abuse. The government also proposes to establish a Criminal Justice Forum which will be representative of all the main criminal justice interests. The Forum will meet twice yearly and will be convened by the Secretary of State. The aim is to provide an opportunity for constructive dialogue on issues of criminal justice.

There will be a period of consultation on the proposals contained in the White Paper ending on 31 July 1996.

GLOSSARY

PREPARED BY REBECCA SAWYER, RESEARCH CONSULTANT

Absolute discharge   granted by the court when a person is found guilty of committing a crime or offence but it is deemed inappropriate to inflict punishment upon the offender. This cannot be granted if the crime has a penalty fixed by statute.

Admonition   a type of disposal used by the court to a person found guilty of a crime or offence, which amounts to being given a warning and then being dismissed. It counts as a conviction.

Advocate   a member of the Scottish Bar.

Advocate depute   appointed by the Lord Advocate and the Solicitor General to assist him with duties. There are 12 advocates depute. Collectively they are known as Crown Counsel. They are members of the Faculty of Advocates.

Advocate, Lord   the senior law officer in Scotland, who is appointed by the Prime Minister. The Lord Advocate is a member of the government, responsible for advising it on legal matters affecting Scotland. He is also the minister in charge of the Lord Advocate's Department, which is responsible for the drafting of all legislation applying to Scotland, and the Crown Office, which is responsible for administering the High Court and sheriff courts.

Agreement of evidence   the Criminal Justice (Scotland) Act 1995 includes the requirement that the prosecutor and the accused, if legally represented, identify matters that may be capable of agreement and to take all reasonable steps to get such agreement before the trial. This will relate to non-controversial evidence.

Appeals   the High Court also sits as the Scottish Court of Criminal Appeals. It sits in Edinburgh and usually with three judges present, although the Criminal Justice (Scotland) Act 1995 reduced this quorum to two in appeals against sentence. It hears appeals against conviction, sentence or both.

Assessment orders   the Children (Scotland) Act 1995 provides social workers with the means of gaining access to children to assess them when parents refuse to co-operate.

Bail   in criminal proceedings, bail acts as a form of security when a person charged with a crime or offence is released before the trial takes place. It seeks to ensure that the accused persons appear in court. Bail does not usually involve handing over sums of money but instead the accused signs a copy of the bail conditions which form an undertaking that he/she will meet. The breach of conditions attached to the bail constitutes a criminal offence, which may be punished by a fine or imprisonment. The Criminal Justice (Scotland) Act 1995 provides that the punishment for breaches of bail is increased to either a fine of up to £1,000 or six months' imprisonment (60 days if in the district court).

Bar   in Scotland, the members of the Faculty of Advocates.

Bill of Advocating   a method of appealing against a procedural irregularity in the course of a trial in an inferior court.

Bill of Suspension   a method of appeal open to the prosecutor and defence if the case is on summary procedure. Suspension is appropriate when the appeal is based either on defects in procedure or on irregular and oppressive conduct on the part of the judge or the prosecutor. It is not open to the prosecutor in solemn procedure.

Case law   law embodied in the decisions of the court.

Caution   (pronounced 'kay-shun')   an order requiring the offender to lodge a sum of money as security for good behaviour in the future. It applies only to common law offences. The sum of money involved must not exceed £2,500 in the district court, or £5,000 in the sheriff summary cases. The 1995 Act provides for the availability of such orders to be extended to solemn procedure with no limit on the sum of money involved. The maximum period over which a caution can be ordered is six months in the district court and 12 months in the sheriff court.

Child protection order   introduced by the Children (Scotland) Act 1995, it involves the Children's Panel and the court. The sheriff court is empowered to make an order which enables the authorities to place a child temporarily in a place of safety. Such an order can only be applied when there is reasonable cause to believe that a child is likely to suffer significant harm and where immediate removal to a place of safety is necessary.

Children's Hearings (or Children's Panel)   founded by the Social Work (Scotland) Act 1968, providing a unique system of juvenile justice and child-care protection for persons under 16 (or up to 18 if they are already under the supervision of the system). The Hearings deal with children who are considered to be in need of compulsory measures of care whether they have offended or have been offended against. They are conducted by a panel of three lay persons. The Reporter is also present at the Hearing. A Hearing is a quasi-judicial tribunal which assesses the needs of the child. A Hearing has the authority to place a child under the

163

compulsory measures of care, which it is the duty of the local authority social work department to implement.

Citation in criminal proceedings, this involves the prosecutor calling to court, in writing, accused persons to answer charges against them as well as specifying on which day this has to be done. A witness in a case is also cited to be at the court on the date when the case is before the court.

Civil law the law which is concerned with the rights and duties of legal or private persons and with settling disputes between such persons.

Clear-up rates the police consider a crime or offence to be 'cleared up' if one or more offenders are apprehended, cited, warned or traced. It does not necessarily mean that a convicton has been secured.

Codified law law that is set down in texts and in statutes.

Common law law which is not based on statute. It includes law based on court decisions and those legal writings which hold authoritative status with the courts and the legal profession.

Community service order this is a requirement for the offender to undertake unpaid work in the community, under the supervision of a social worker. The offender must consent to the programme. The minimum number of hours is 40 and the maximum has been increased in the Criminal Justice (Scotland) Act 1995 to 300 hours (from a previous limit of 240).

Compensation order The Criminal Justice (Scotland) Act 1980 gave the Scottish criminal courts the power to order offenders to pay compensation to victims for loss or injury resulting from the crime. The orders are usually imposed alongside a fine.

Complaint a document which begins the summary criminal

proceedings in a sheriff or district court and also explains the charge that is being made.

Corroboration   in criminal proceedings, evidence that is used to confirm the already existing evidence. In Scots law a conviction cannot be secured on the evidence of one person alone. That evidence must be corroborated from another source.

Countermand   the cancellation of a citation to attend court.

Court of Appeal   the highest court in Scotland. It sits in Edinburgh and hears appeals from the district and sheriff courts as well as the High Court. It hears appeals against conviction, sentence, or both on the grounds that there has been a miscarriage of justice. There is no appeal to the House of Lords in criminal cases.

Crown   in relation to criminal proceedings this refers to Her Majesty's government.

Crown Agent   the most senior official within the Crown Office.

Crown Office   is under the control of the Lord Advocate, who is responsible for the public prosecution of crime in Scotland.

Dark figure of crime   a term used in relation to crime statistics, referring to the difference between the number of crimes committed and the number of crimes recorded by the police.

Detention   the Criminal Justice (Scotland) Act 1980 gave the police the power to detain a person for limited periods without arrest or charge. This term also refers to the imprisonment of offenders under 21.

Diet   the meeting of the court for actually hearing the case.

District court   introduced by the District Courts (Scotland) Act 1975 for each district or islands area. These courts are concerned with the less serious criminal offences and are presided over either by justices of the peace or by stipendiary magistrates. The court can only deal with summary criminal matters and can impose maximum sentences of 60 days' imprisonment and/or a £2,500 fine.

Diversion   the process of directing offenders away from traditional penal sanctions where prosecution is not considered to be in the public interest. It can include social work assistance and reparation and mediation schemes.

Exclusion order   the Children (Scotland) Act 1995 introduced this order aimed at excluding abusers from the home. It aims to protect children who are victims of significant harm. Such an order can only be granted by the sheriff on application.

Fatal accident inquiry   an inquiry which may occur when there is a death in the course of employment, or in custody, or a death which is otherwise sudden, suspicious or unexplained. It is initiated by the procurator fiscal and conducted by the sheriff.

First diet   this is a mandatory diet for sheriff and jury trials requiring the attendance of the accused. The purpose is to ascertain whether the case is likely to proceed to trial having regard to the state of preparation of the prosecutor and the accused and the extent to which agreement of evidence has been sought. The accused is required to plead at the first diet. If the accused pleads guilty then the court can dispose of the case or adjourn for sentence to be passed. If the accused pleads not guilty the case will be continued to the trial diet, the date of which appears on the indictment.

Fiscal fines   an alternative to prosecution. A fiscal can offer a fine for all offences that are triable summarily. The Criminal Justice (Scotland) Act 1995 provides for a sliding scale of fines rather than the previous system where the fine was fixed at £25. These new measures came into effect in April 1996.

Guardianship order   when the court places a mentally disturbed individual under the control of a guardian, rather than a hospital.

High Court of Justiciary   the supreme criminal court in Scotland. It sits in Edinburgh and a number of other towns on a circuit basis dealing with first instance criminal business. It only hears cases on indictment and has exclusive jurisdiction over very serious crimes, including murder, rape and treason. It also serves as a Court of Appeal, sitting in Edinburgh only.

Hospital Order   a means of detaining a mentally disturbed offender in a hospital.

Indictment   a document written in the name of the Lord Advocate which contains an accusation of a serious crime. All prosecutions held before a jury proceed on indictment; this is known as solemn procedure.

Intermediate diet   the Criminal Justice (Scotland) Act 1995 requires intermediate diets to take place in all summary criminal cases, rather than just in sheriff and jury cases (see 'First diet'). These are sittings which take place before the actual trial takes place, and they aim to establish matters which can be agreed before the trial.

Judicial examination   a formal procedure by which the accused, appearing before the sheriff and the procurator fiscal, is given an early opportunity to offer a defence. The accused does not have to make any comment, but failure to do so may be adversely commented on at trial. The new provisions in the Criminal Justice (Scotland) Act 1995 permit questions to include those directed towards eliciting an admission from the accused.

Justice Clerk, Lord   appointed by the Crown, the Lord

Justice Clerk is positioned second in the hierarchy of Scottish judges who constitute the Court of Session and High Court of the Justiciary. The position involves acting as a depute for the Lord President when necessary.

Justice General, Lord   the judge who presides over the High Court of Justiciary. The office was merged with that of Lord President of the Court of Session, the senior Scottish Judge, in 1823.

Justice of the Peace   a lay person, appointed by the Secretary of State for Scotland, who presides over a district court. They are effectively the 'judges' of these courts even though they are not legally trained.

Kilbrandon Report   the result of an inquiry instigated by the government to examine the issue of young people and criminal justice. The Kilbrandon Committee reported in 1964 and had a profound effect on the juvenile justice system in Scotland. The Report suggested that the existing juvenile courts were unsuitable for dealing with children and was the basis on which the Children's Hearings system was established, emphasising a shift towards treatment and care and away from punishment.

Legal aid   a statutory scheme which provides legal advice or representation to those with few resources. The financial support is determined individually for each case, and it is likely that the recipient will have to make some form of contribution to the final costs.

Lord Advocate   see 'Advocate, Lord'.

Lord Justice Clerk   see 'Justice Clerk, Lord'.

Lord Justice General   see 'Justice General, Lord'.

Mediation   an alternative to prosecution which involves the accused, the victim and a third party trying to reach some form of agreement about the offence committed.

Not proven   a verdict unique to the Scottish criminal justice system, which is available as a third verdict together with 'not guilty' and 'guilty'. It has the same fundamental effect as the verdict 'not guilty' in that the accused is acquitted.

Parole   the discretionary early release of a long-term prisoner on licence and subject to conditions (particularly social work supervision) on the recommendation of the Parole Board for Scotland. The Secretary of State can release a prisoner on parole only on the recommendation of the Board, and in the case of a prisoner subject to a life sentence for murder he must also consult the judiciary.

Petition   the initial document in solemn procedure that sets out the name, designation and address of the accused and the charge; it also asks for the necessary warrants.

Plea in mitigation   once a person has been found guilty, either the accused or their lawyer may plead that there is a reason why the maximum penalty should not be imposed.

Pleading diet   first court-calling in summary procedure.

Precognition   an oral examination of a person who may be required to give evidence at either civil or criminal hearings. The procurator fiscal takes the statements of the most important witnesses.

Preliminary diet   this is similar to a first diet in sheriff and jury proceedings but is only heard in High Court proceedings where either the Crown or defence give written notice that they wish to raise certain preliminary pleas or other matters before the trial diet.

Probation   in criminal proceedings, a community disposal to which offenders must give their consent. It seeks to reduce the risk of reoffending by combining supervision and control with help to deal with problems. Probation orders may last for between six months and three years.

Procurator fiscal procurators fiscal are the public prosecutors in both the district and sheriff courts. Once a crime has been reported to the police, the procurator fiscal has the discretion to decide whether or not to prosecute. They are also responsible for the instigation of fatal accident inquiries.

Remand where an accused person is placed in custody or on bail at the start of criminal proceedings.

Reparation an option normally used as an alternative to prosecution which entails the accused making some form of amends to the victim in an attempt to compensate for the offence.

Reporter to the Children's Panel in the context of juvenile justice, this is the person appointed to investigate cases of children referred to him/her, to decide whether a child is in need of compulsory measures of care and whether he/she should be referred to a Children's Hearing. Reporters had been appointed by the Regional and Islands Councils, but from 1 April 1996 they are appointed by the Scottish Children's Reporter Administration.

Scottish Prison Service an executive agency of the Scottish Office, headed by a chief executive, a civil servant, who is responsible to the Secretary of State. The headquarters are based in Edinburgh and the agency is responsible for running the prisons on behalf of the Secretary of State for Scotland, who is responsible to parliament.

Sheriff the judge who presides over the sheriff court. To become a sheriff, one must have been a professional lawyer who has practised for at least 10 years as a solicitor or as an advocate. There are 97 sheriffs in Scotland. The senior judge in each of the six sheriffdoms is called the Sheriff Principal.

Sheriff clerk the clerk to the sheriff court, who is a civil servant.

Sheriff court   the court below the High Court. It exercises both solemn and summary jurisdiction. There are 49 sheriff court districts.

Solemn procedure   the procedure whereby a person accused of a serious crime on indictment is brought to a trial with a judge and a jury which consists of 15 members. This is confined to the sheriff court and the High Court.

Solicitor-General   a law officer of the Crown and deputy to the Lord Advocate. Also a member of the government.

Stipendiary magistrate   a legally qualified judge appointed by the local authority who presides over the district court and has the same summary criminal sentencing power as a sheriff (that is, three years' imprisonment and a £5,000 fine).

Summary procedure   the procedure whereby a person accused of committing a crime is brought before a sheriff, magistrate or justice sitting alone. There is no jury and it is confined to district and sheriff courts.

Supervised attendance order   a disposal which provides an alternative to custody for those offenders who default on payment of a fine. Orders require offenders to undertake constructive activities, including educational programmes and unpaid work, for between 10 and 100 hours. The Criminal Justice (Scotland) Act 1995 contains provisions to allow SAOs to be used for 16- and 17-year-old offenders in place of a fine where the court considers they would be unable to pay. The Act also contains provisions which aim to remove custody as a sanction for fine default.

Trial diet   the final diet when the accused comes to court, and, unless postponed or abandoned, the case proceeds to a verdict.

Warrant   a written document from the court giving authority to carry out certain actions, such as arresting a named person or searching a specified place.

Young Offenders Institution   young persons aged from 16 to under 21 are sent here, rather than to an adult prison, when they receive a custodial sentence.

BIBLIOGRAPHY

Anderson, S. and Leitch, S. (1994), *Scottish Crime Survey: First Results*, The Scottish Office.

Business Plan: 1989–92 (1989), The Scottish Prison Service.

Continuity Through Cooperation (1990), The Scottish Prison Service and the Social Work Services Group.

Corporate Plan (1993), The Scottish Prison Service.

Crime and Punishment (1996), The Scottish Office.

Criminal Statistics, Scotland (1975), The Scottish Office.

Firm and Fair (1994), The Scottish Office.

Inquiry into the Removal of Children from Orkney (1991), The Scottish Office.

Moore, G. and Wood, C. (1992), *Social Work and Criminal Law in Scotland*, Mercat Press.

Opportunity and Responsibility: Developing New Approaches to the Management of the Long-Term Prison System in Scotland (1990), The Scottish Prison Service.

Preventing Crime Together in Scotland: A Strategy for the 90s (1992), The Scottish Office.

Scotland's Children: Proposals for Child Care Policy and Law (1993), The Scottish Office.

Further Reading

Criminal Law in Scotland

Gordon, G. (1978, supplements 1992), *The Criminal Law of Scotland*, W. Green.

McCall Smith, R. and Sheldon, D. (1992), *Scots Criminal Law*, W. Green.

Criminal Procedure

Renton, R. and Brown, H. (1984), *Criminal Procedure according to the Law of Scotland*, W. Green.

Public Prosecution

Tombs, J. and Moody, S. (1993), *Alternatives to Prosecution, Criminal Law Review* pp357–367.

Criminal Courts

Stewart, A. (1990), *The Scottish Criminal Courts in Action*, Butterworths and Co.

Prisons

Coyle, A. (1991), *Inside: Rethinking Scotland's Prisons*, Scottish Child.

Children's Hearings

Martin, F. and Murray, K. (1977), *The Scottish Juvenile Justice System,* Scottish Academic Press.

INDEX

Printed in Scotland for The Stationery Office Limited by CC No 13129 30C 01/97